The Craft of Furniture Making

The Craft of Furniture Making

David Johnston

B T Batsford Ltd   London

This book is dedicated to my wife, Audrey, and my daughter, Hilary.

Illustrations: John Williams

Photography: Tony Anderson

© David Johnston 1979
First published 1979
Second edition 1981

ISBN 0 7134 1547 9 (paperback)

Printed by The Anchor Press Ltd, Tiptree
for the publishers B T Batsford Limited
4 Fitzhardinge Street, London W1H 0AH

Contents

Introduction

We live in an age of synthetic materials and mechanisation. Most furniture today is made in factories from various forms of reconstituted wood covered with thin veneers of decorative hardwood. Much of this furniture is well designed and well constructed but it lacks the quality of hand-fashioned natural wood. The man who makes his own furniture not only has the satisfaction of producing something of character with a practical and lasting value, but he also acquires a manual skill, which is lacking in most people's lives today and derives a pleasure from working with a material which is variable and versatile, and which has a natural beauty.

This book was written by an amateur for amateurs, and is based almost entirely upon the personal experience and work of the author. It is not a complete woodworking or cabinet-making manual, but is an attempt to explain what the amateur needs to know in order to produce a useful range of good quality furniture using only hand tools. With the exception of the work bench, which is described in Chapter 8, there are no detailed plans of particular pieces of furniture. Instead, the basic techniques and methods of construction are described in detail so that the reader may develop his skill and work from his own designs. The author believes that anyone working seriously with wood needs, in addition to a knowledge of the basic techniques, some understanding of the nature and properties of his raw material and tools, and these aspects of cabinet-making are dealt with in the book.

As with most activities, competence in furniture making comes with practice, but successful results depend also upon the worker's attitude and motivation. An amateur is unlikely to have the ability of the professional cabinet-maker, but most people who are prepared to try hard enough and to take sufficient care are capable of making furniture which will give them lasting satisfaction and pleasure.

I am most grateful to John Williams, who drew the diagrams, Tony Anderson, who took the photographs, and to the following people and organizations who have read the text and suggested improvements: M Withers Green, J Brazier and J Boxall of the Princes Risborough Laboratory of The Building Research Establishment, J Sainsbury of Record Ridgway Tools, S D Holmes of Borden (UK) Ltd, English Abrasives Limited, C W Loftus of L G Wilkinson Ltd, D G McKay of Berger Paints, and R P Sharphouse of the Timber Research and Development Association. Record Ridgway Tools, Stanley Tools Ltd and Spear & Jackson (Tools) Ltd provided the photographs and diagrams of tools shown in Chapter 2, and the Building Research Establishment supplied figures 3 and 4 which are Crown copyright.

Finally, I am indebted to my wife who was responsible for all the typing and secretarial work and without whose help none of the furniture illustrated in the book would have been glued together.

D J

CHAPTER 1 **The raw material**

Wood is a complex, versatile and variable material. Its variability gives it beauty but also imposes limitations on its use. It is not necessary for the furniture maker to have a profound knowledge of the biology of wood but some understanding of its structure and properties helps him to exploit its good qualities and to accommodate its bad ones. There is a relationship between growth and structure and between structure and properties and, at the risk of some over-simplification, these relationships are briefly described in this chapter.

Growth
The stem of a tree is a gentle paraboloid with, generally, a swelling at the base which becomes more pronounced with age and which, in some tropical species, may take the form of massive buttresses extending several metres up the tree. This shape is shown in an exaggerated form in figure 1.

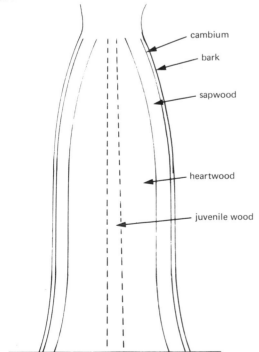

cambium

bark

sapwood

heartwood

juvenile wood

1   The stem of a tree

Just below the bark and forming a complete sheath around all the branches and the stem is a thin layer of tissue known as the cambium which produces wood cells towards the centre of the tree and bark cells towards the outside. The wood cells of the stem perform three functions. They provide mechanical support for the crown, they conduct water and nutrients from the roots to the leaves and they store food made by the leaves.

Water conduction and food storage occur in the sapwood. This is an outermost zone of wood which, depending upon the species, age and condition of growth of the tree, may be about 12 mm ($\frac{1}{2}$ in) to 75 mm (3 in) wide. Inside the sapwood is the heartwood. This is generally more durable than the sapwood, contains less moisture and is usually darker in colour although in some species the sapwood and heartwood are visually indistinguishable.

In the temperate regions growth is almost entirely restricted to the spring and summer. In most coniferous and some broadleaved species, such as oak and ash, the wood cells produced in the spring are different from those produced in the summer and there is a very conspicuous growth ring. In other species, such as beech and sycamore, there is far less contrast in the cell structure, and growth rings, although present, are less obvious. Spring wood is often referred to as early wood and summer wood as late wood.

In the tropics, where growth is often more or less continuous throughout the year, the annual rings cannot easily be identified unless there is a pronounced dry season in which case some cyclical pattern of growth may be detected.

As the stem of a tree grows it encloses the branches which form knots in the wood. While the branch is still living the enclosed knot is, structurally, part of the stem and is known as a live knot. But after a branch has died the dead wood enclosed by the stem has no structural connection with the surrounding tissue and is known as a dead knot. In conifers, dead knots often fall out after the tree has been felled and sawn, while in broadleaves they are less common and tend to rot rather than fall out.

For any given species the pattern of growth can, to a considerable extent, be influenced by the forester who can select, for example, for vigour, straightness and branching habit in his tree breeding programme, and who can influence growth rate by his choice of planting site and by the use of fertilizers. Diameter growth and branchiness, but not height growth, can be influenced by spacing so that trees planted wider apart, or given more space by the removal of their neighbours, become larger in girth and more tapered and have thicker branches, and hence larger knots, than trees grown more closely together. Much of the wood used in furniture making, however, comes from natural or semi-natural forests in which the growth of individual trees has been little, if at all, influenced by management practices.

The new cells generally grow from the cambium in an approximately vertical direction more or less parallel with the long axis of the stem. Sometimes, however, they grow at an angle, thus forming a spiral round the tree. This is illustrated in figure 2.

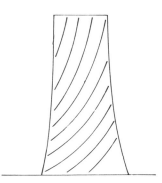

2   Spiral growth

Spiral grain is more common in some species than others and frequently occurs, for example, in Sweet chestnut. In some tropical species, such as sapele, the direction of the spiral changes every few years. This is known as interlocked grain which produces a striped or banded effect on a planed radial surface.

Wood from near the centre of the tree, known as juvenile wood, is less dense, less strong and more knotty than the more mature wood and in conifers tends to have more spiral grain. The boundary between the two is gradual but the juvenile characteristics are only pronounced in the ten to twenty annual rings in the centre of the stem.

All wood is composed of small cells the principal structural material of which is cellulose which forms the cell walls. This is reinforced with hemicellulose and lignin which add strength and rigidity. Various other chemicals occur in different species and these affect the colour, smell and durability of the wood. There are significant differences in structure between conifers, such as pine and spruce, and broadleaves, such as oak and birch.

The wood of conifers is usually referred to as softwood and that of broadleaves as hardwood. These descriptions are generally valid but some hardwoods such as poplar or obeche are softer than some softwoods such as yew or Pitch pine. With the exception of yew, the principal high quality furniture timbers are all hardwoods.

The structure of conifers
There are two types of cell in conifers. Most of them are fibres (or tracheids) which serve both to conduct water and nutrients and to provide mechanical strength. The others are food storage cells (or parenchyma) which occur in very small quantities. The fibres formed at the beginning of the growing season are relatively larger in diameter and have thinner walls than those formed later in the year. They range in length from 3 mm (almost $\frac{1}{8}$ in) to 7 mm (just over $\frac{1}{4}$ in) with an average length of 3.5 mm (just over $\frac{1}{8}$ in). Their length is about one hundred times their diameter.

The boundary between the early and late wood may be abrupt as in larch, Douglas fir and most pines or gradual as in the firs and spruces.

For any given species density, which is closely correlated with strength, depends upon cell diameter and cell-wall thickness and upon the proportions of early and late wood. Fast-growing trees have wider annual rings and tend to have larger and thinner-walled and therefore weaker fibres than slower-growing trees. Fast growth does not necessarily, however, result in weak wood of low density. On some favourable sites and under good growing conditions trees continue to grow until late into the season and produce a relatively large proportion of strong, thick-walled, late wood fibres.

The storage cells, which are inconspicuous in conifers, occur among the fibres or in the form of rays extending radially through the wood. The rays are typically only one cell wide but are several cells deep. They are barely visible to the naked eye.

Many conifers contain resin cells or resin ducts which give the characteristic resin smell to the wood and which, on occasions, make the wood sticky to work.

The structure of broadleaves

The wood cells in broadleaves are generally shorter than those in conifers and there is greater differentiation between the cells which conduct water and nutrients and those which provide strength and rigidity. The storage cells are similar in structure and function to those in conifers but they are more abundant and more variable.

The conducting cells, which are called vessels, range in diameter from 0.02 mm (less than $\frac{1}{1000}$ in) to 0.5 mm (about $\frac{1}{64}$ in) so that in some species they are large enough to be seen easily by the naked eye. They always occur in vertical series which form tube-like structures extending vertically for some distance in the tree.

In most species there is little contrast in the size or pattern of the vessels across the growth ring and these are known as diffuse-porous species. In some species, however, the transition from large thin-walled early-wood vessels to smaller thicker-walled late-wood vessels is abrupt and the early-wood vessels form a series of distinct rings which are clearly visible on the end grain of the wood. These are the ring-porous species which include oak, elm and Sweet chestnut. In oak, for example, the diameter of the early-wood vessels can be as much as ten times that of the late wood. Unlike most species faster growth in the ring-porous group is always associated with denser and stronger wood, because of the larger proportion of the denser late wood. Ring-porous wood and diffuse-porous wood are shown in figures 3a and 3b.

The fibres in broadleaves are similar to the late-wood fibres in conifers although they are shorter, averaging 1 mm (about $\frac{1}{25}$ in) to 1.5 mm ($\frac{1}{16}$ in) in length. The thickness of the fibre wall and its physical and chemical properties are major factors in determining the strength and working properties of the wood.

The storage tissue occurs in various patterns amongst the vessels and fibres, sometimes forming distinct bands, and sometimes distributed throughout the wood. It also forms radial rays which are generally larger and more conspicuous than those in conifers. The rays are usually several

3a Ring-porous wood (oak)

3b Diffuse-porous wood (beech)

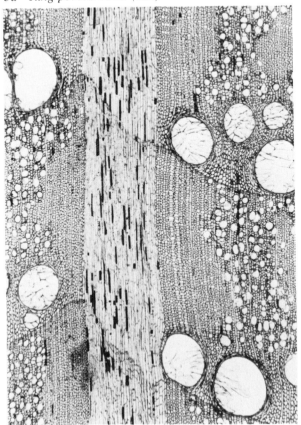

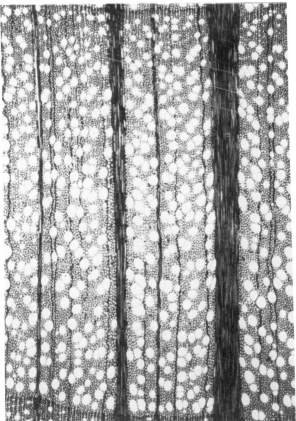

cells wide and in some woods, such as oak, are many cells deep forming a major feature on radial surfaces.

A few broadleaved species contain resin ducts and the storage tissue of many species contains crystals, usually of calcium oxalate and, less frequently, of silica.

Grain, texture and figure

Grain

Grain is the direction of the fibres relative to the long axis of the tree or of a particular piece of wood. Straight grain is self-explanatory but there are various forms of irregular grain some of which have a decorative value. A not uncommon form of irregularity is spiral grain which has no decorative value except when it is interlocked (page 10). Wavy grain, of which fiddle-back maple is an example, gives a ripple effect on tangential surfaces while an unusual growth malformation in the cambium of some species, such as maple and birch, causes the cells to grow into a series of small depressions giving a bird's-eye pattern. Sloping

grain occurs when timber is not sawn parallel with the long axis of the tree and is particularly common when the tree has a pronounced butt swell or when the stem is bowed. Knots are also a cause of irregularity. Interlocked grain and fiddle-back grain are shown in figures 4a and 4b.

Texture

Texture in hardwoods depends primarily upon the size and distribution of the wood cells and to a much lesser extent upon the rays. Wood with large vessels and large rays, such as oak, is said to be coarse-textured, while wood with small vessels and insignificant rays is said to be fine-textured. Texture in conifers depends mainly upon the contrast between early and late wood and upon the rate of growth.

Figure

Figure is the pattern produced on the longitudinal surface of the wood by the arrangement of the various forms of tissue, such as vessels, fibres, storage cells and rays, by the grain of the wood and by the annual rings. Figure depends to a considerable extent upon the direction in which

4a   Interlocked grain (sapele)

4b   Fiddle-back grain (maple)

wood is sawn. Rays, for example, only form a major feature if they are large and if the wood is sawn radially (quarter sawn), while some decorative effects of irregular grain are only apparent on tangential surfaces.

Defects

Knots

Knots cause irregular grain and reduce the strength of the wood. As well as being less strong than straight-grained wood, the irregular grain is difficult to work and tends to tear when planed. Knots are particularly troublesome if they occur where joints have to be cut. It is quite impracticable to cut mortices and undesirable to cut tenons or dovetail joints through large knots. But perhaps the most serious disadvantage of knots is their tendency to cause wood to distort with changes in moisture content.

Very knotty timber is sometimes used for decorative panels where strength is a minor consideration, and knots are of relatively little importance in large-dimensioned structural timber. Moderately knotty timber can be used for softwood furniture and for utility furniture which is to be painted provided no knots or knot clusters form a large proportion of the cross-sectional area of any structural member. For fine furniture, however, knots have to be considered a serious defect.

Irregular grain

Irregular grain has been discussed on page 12 Some irregular grain such as interlocked or bird's-eye grain is considered to be a desirable decorative feature despite the fact that it is difficult to plane and requires careful finishing to achieve a smooth surface. Other forms of irregular grain, such as spiral, knotty or sloping grain, have no merit but considerable disadvantages. They are all liable to cause serious distortion with changes in moisture content, and wood with pronounced spiral or sloping grain should not be used in furniture making and particularly not in large or thin sheets.

Reaction wood

A stem or branch which is not growing vertically produces reaction wood. In conifers the reaction wood occurs on the underside of the leaning stem and is known as compression wood while in broadleaves it occurs on the upper side and is known as tension wood. Reaction wood is generally weaker than normal wood and, unlike normal wood, it has a very high longitudinal shrinkage which causes planks to bow or spring

with changes in moisture content. Compression wood is usually easy to recognise because it is darker in colour than the surrounding wood and tends to occur in longitudinal streaks. There is usually, also, a lack of contrast in colour between the early and late wood. Tension wood, on the other hand, can be paler or darker than normal wood and tends to be rather woolly and brittle to work. Another indication of the likely presence of reaction wood is very eccentric growth as seen on the cross section of a log. This is shown in figure 5.

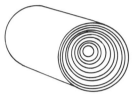

5   Eccentric growth associated with reaction wood

Brittleheart

Brittleheart is a defect which is liable to occur in the centre of fast-growing, low to medium-density tropical broadleaved species such as African mahogany. In a large tree the outer part of the stem is in a state of tension which the central portion may be unable to withstand. This leads to numerous minute failures in the cell walls of the wood. Wood with brittleheart has a somewhat carroty texture which is easy to detect. It should not be used in furniture.

Juvenile wood

The inner ten to twenty rings of a tree consist of juvenile wood. This is less dense and less strong than the older wood outside it and sometimes the grain tends to be more spiral, especially in conifers. It is therefore inadvisable to use small pieces of wood for furniture making if they are cut from the centre of the tree.

Properties

Response to sawing

There are some internal stresses in most large pieces of wood and if they are sawn into smaller pieces some of the stresses are released. This results in distortion which is quite distinct from the seasoning movements discussed in the next section. It cannot, therefore, be assumed that a straight line scribed longitudinally down the centre of a piece of wood will still be straight when the wood has been sawn into two pieces.

Response to changes in moisture content

Wood achieves an equilibrium condition in

centrally heated homes at a moisture content of about 12 per cent of the dry weight of the wood. This may fall to about 10 per cent in the winter when the house is heated and rise to about 14 per cent in the autumn. When freshly felled the moisture content may be more than 100 per cent and when completely air dry, under cover in a temperate climate, the moisture content falls to about 20 per cent in the winter and about 15 per cent in the summer.

Wood does not begin to shrink until the moisture content has fallen to about 30 per cent. Below this level shrinkage is approximately proportional to moisture content so that the shrinkage from 30 per cent to 20 per cent moisture content is the same as that between 20 per cent and 10 per cent. Shrinkage in the tangential plane is 1.5 to 2 times that in the radial plane while in the longitudinal plane it is almost negligible, except, as mentioned above, in reaction wood where it may be considerable. As an example, normal English oak in drying from 14 per cent to 10 per cent moisture content shrinks about 1.9 per cent tangentially and 1.0 per cent radially.

Most timber is liable to split or distort to some extent while it is being seasoned and with low quality logs or with some unstable species the damage can be very serious. It can greatly be reduced by careful stacking and seasoning but is most effectively prevented by kiln drying under controlled conditions of temperature and humidity. Much of the advantage of kiln drying is lost if the wood is subsequently exposed to a high level of humidity, especially if it is not constrained but allowed to move freely.

After wood has been dried to an equilibrium moisture content and is in service, it continues to shrink and swell as the ambient humidity and hence the moisture content of the wood changes. The movement is, however, appreciably less for a given change in moisture content than when the

wood was originally drying from the freshly felled condition. The pattern of shrinkage in wood which is free of defects is shown in figure 6.

Quarter (radially) sawn planks shrink uniformly and do not change their shape whereas flat (tangentially) sawn planks tend to cup towards the outside of the tree.

The various defects described on page 13 cause additional distortion as the moisture content of the wood changes. Spiral grain leads to twisting, and reaction wood and sloping grain to bowing and springing in the longitudinal plane. Planks containing a significant proportion of juvenile wood are also liable to bow or spring. These forms of distortion are shown in figure 7.

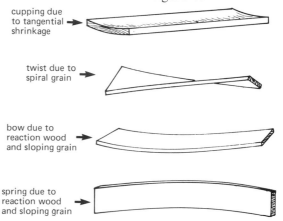

cupping due to tangential shrinkage

twist due to spiral grain

bow due to reaction wood and sloping grain

spring due to reaction wood and sloping grain

7   *Wood distortion*

As wood is seasoned the outer layer dries first and comes under a tension stress but is restrained from shrinking by the wetter interior portion, rather as happens when brittleheart is formed. The outer layer is said to become case-hardened and it inhibits and delays the drying of the centre of the wood. Case-hardening is aggravated by rapid drying and is more likely to occur with thick pieces of wood. Some degree of case-hardening is, however, very common in any wood dried naturally and furniture components which are cut to approximate dimensions and then left for some time in a heated house are likely to become case-hardened. If they have any inherent tendency to distort they will do so when they are subsequently planed to their final dimensions and the case-hardened surface removed. A case-hardened piece of wood may bow slightly when one face is planed but subsequently return to its original shape when the opposite face has also been planed.

It is one of the difficulties of the amateur that he

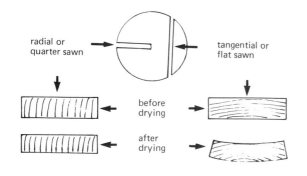

radial or quarter sawn

tangential or flat sawn

before drying

after drying

6   *Wood shrinkage*

often has to make a piece of furniture over a long period of time. This means that components which are planed carefully to shape and size may have moved or distorted slightly when the time comes to assemble and glue the completed work. Wood which has distorted can usually be straightened and this is discussed in the next section.

Seasoned wood is stronger than wet wood and it also glues better. At about the equilibrium moisture content in houses the stiffness of wood (see the next section) is increased by about 2 per cent for each 1 per cent decrease in moisture content.

The strength of wood

Timber possesses various different strength qualities. It may withstand a sustained load or a sudden impact or resist compression parallel with or across the grain. It may be hard and it may resist bending. Of these qualities the more important for furniture making are the ability to resist bending (stiffness) and hardness. There is a correlation, but not a simple one, between stiffness and strength (the ability to resist breaking under a load).

The stiffness of a beam is proportional to its width and to the cube of its depth while the breaking strength is proportional to its width but to the square of the depth. Stiffness is inversely proportional to the cube of the span, while breaking strength is inversely proportional to the span. These relationships are illustrated in figure 8.

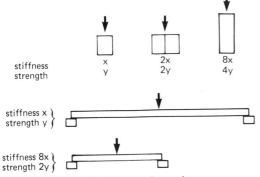

8   *The strength and stiffness of wood*

Very soft woods are not suitable for furniture making. Furniture needs to be able to withstand a certain amount of ill-treatment without denting and bruising. Although pine is quite widely used for furniture it is easily grooved and dented unless protected by a hard surface such as a polyurethane lacquer.

No timber is perfectly elastic so that if it is subjected to a load it never completely recovers its original shape. The longer the load is applied the greater will be the permanent distortion. This quality may be exploited to re-shape wood which has become distorted for any reason. If, for example, a piece of wood has become twisted, it may be staightened by cramping it for a period of time to a firm base over a diagonal rod, such as a broom handle, so that it is twisted in the opposite direction.

This straightening is a matter of trial and error but as the wood is not weakened by the process the movement can be reversed if necessary. One of the drawer fronts of the chest illustrated on page 46 was straightened in this way over a period of about two weeks. The process can be hastened by putting wet towels on the concave surface, but if this is done the wood must be held rigid after it has been straightened while it regains its equilibrium moisture content.

Manufactured panels

There are five main types of manufactured board. These are particle or chipboard, blockboard, laminboard, plywood and hardboard. The amateur may find all these materials useful in joinery work such as shelving, fitted cupboards, or kitchen fitments but, with the exception of plywood, they have no place in good quality hand-made furniture. Plywood is the exception because it is particularly appropriate for the bottoms of drawers and for the backs of cabinets, where, if firmly fixed, it behaves as a very narrow but very deep beam of tremendous stiffness. These materials are discussed in more detail in Chapter 18.

Furniture timbers

Over the centuries the number of species of wood used in furniture making has steadily increased as new sources of supply have been opened up. At the same time the popularity of some of them has changed with fashion. In Europe, oak was the prime furniture timber for many centuries. Walnut was first used in the sixteenth century and became important in the seventeenth and early eighteenth centuries when oak, beech and walnut were the principal species used by cabinet makers. Mahogany from Cuba and Honduras was introduced into Europe and North America in the first half of the eighteenth century, while rosewood from Brazil and India and satinwood from Ceylon and the West Indies became popular on both sides of the Atlantic towards the end of the eighteenth century. Yew, the only really high quality coniferous species, was first used widely in the eighteenth century. During the nineteenth century the number of available species increased steadily but only those which were easily accessible and of high quality, such as the African mahoganies, sapele, afrormosia, iroko and teak were considered worthwhile harvesting. As the highest-quality timbers become increasingly scarce and expensive, attempts are being made to harvest a larger number of the numerous species which grow naturally in the tropical forests, not only in Africa and the Far East but also in South America. Some of these species are of high quality but because they occur in small quantities and in relatively inaccessible regions it has been impracticable to market them in the past. There are so many species in South America, for example, that they may not be marketed individually but in groups of species having roughly comparable properties.

The more important temperate and tropical furniture species are briefly described below in alphabetical order. A relative rating is given for stiffness, stability in use and hardness, I denoting above average, II denoting average and III denoting below average.

Hardwoods

Afrormosia (Pericopsis elata, West Africa)
A fine textured, medium yellow-brown timber with interlocked grain which gives a banded figure (page 10), it is similar to teak in properties and appearance but is finer grained and, containing less silica, does not blunt tools so quickly. It is a high class furniture timber. Stiffness II, stability II, hardness I/II.

Ash (Fraxinus excelsior, Europe)
This is a very pale, straight-grained, ring-porous wood; the bands of early-wood vessels give a slight decorative figure on flat-sawn planks. Stiffness II, stability II/III, hardness I/II.

Beech (Fagus sylvatica, Europe)
A pale-coloured, fine-textured and straight-grained wood with distinctly visible rays, it is a somewhat characterless furniture timber but works easily. Stiffness II, stability III, hardness I/II.

Cherry (Prunus avium, Europe)
A fine-textured, straight-grained, pale brown wood, it is rarely available in large sizes but is suitable for small cabinet and inlay work. Stiffness II, stability II, hardness II.

Chestnut, Sweet (Castanea sativa, Europe)
The timber closely resembles flat-sawn oak but has no obvious rays. It works and finishes well and has a pleasing colour and texture. The wood from old trees is very liable to have a spiral grain. Stiffness II/III, stability II, hardness II.

Elm, English (Ulmus procera, Europe)
This medium-brown timber has a coarse and often interlocked grain which gives it an attractive figure. It is difficult to season and distorts when worked. Dutch elm *(Ulmus hollandica)*, Wych elm *(Ulmus glabra)* and American elm *(Ulmus americana)* are similar to English elm in appearance but are stronger and usually straighter grained. This makes them easier to season and work but they lack the pronounced figure of English elm. Elm is a very suitable wood for cottage-type furniture and can be used for fine furniture if it is very carefully seasoned. Stiffness II/III, stability III, hardness II.

Iroko (Chlorophora excelsa, East and West Africa)
Iroko is a dark brown, relatively coarse-textured timber with some irregular and interlocked grain. It superficially resembles teak but can be identified by its coarser and more irregular grain and by its darker colour. It is a rather crude looking timber for fine furniture. Stiffness II, stability I, hardness II.

Mahogany, African (Khaya spp, West Africa)
There are several similar species of khaya marketed as African mahogany. The timber is variable in quality and properties but is always a pleasant pale pinkish-brown colour with a moderately fine texture and somewhat interlocked grain. It is reasonably easy to work but requires care if the grain is particularly irregular. Stiffness III, stability II, hardness II/III.

Mahogany, Honduras (Swietenia macrophylla, Honduras) and Mahogany, Cuban (Swietenia mahagoni, Cuba)
These two species provided the classical furniture timber of the eighteenth and nineteenth centuries. They are similar to African mahogany but have a more delicate appearance. Honduras mahogany is expensive and Cuban mahogany is unobtainable. Stiffness II, stability I, hardness II.

Oak, European (Quercus petraea, Europe, and Quercus robur, Europe) and Oak, American white (mainly Quercus alba, North America)
The timbers of the two European oaks are indistinguishable and they closely resemble American white oak in appearance and properties. Oak is a pale fawn wood with a straight grain and a fairly coarse texture. Its most distinctive feature is the presence of very deep, silvery coloured rays on radial surfaces. When free from knots and other

defects it works well. Stiffness I/II, stability II/III, hardness I/II.

Ramin (Gonystylus spp, Malaya)
A very pale wood with a fine texture and a straight or sometimes slightly interlocked grain. It is not suitable for the exterior parts of furniture because it entirely lacks character, but it works well and is suitable for such purposes as drawer sides. Stiffness II, stability III, hardness II.

Rosewood (Dalbergia spp, Brazil and India)
There are a number of species of dalbergia marketed as rosewood. The most common is Dalbergia latifolia from India which is a rich brown wood with dark markings, having a fine and straight grain. It works very well and takes an extremely fine finish but tends to blunt cutting edges fairly quickly. It is said to be rather difficult to season. The strongly contrasting colour of freshly cut rosewood can appear rather crude to some people but it quickly mellows to a rich brown and black and is one of the most handsome of all furniture timbers. Stiffness I, stability I, hardness I.

Sapele (Entandophragma cylindricum, West Africa)
Sapele is harder, darker and stronger than the African mahoganies and has a very pronounced banded or striped effect on radial surfaces due to its regularly interlocked grain. Apart from some difficulty in planing it works well. Stiffness II, stability II, hardness II.

Teak (Tectona grandis, India and Burma)
A golden brown timber having a medium texture and a straight grain, it is somewhat variable in appearance and sometimes shows slightly darker markings. It is very strong in all respects for its weight. Teak is easy to work apart from the fact that it contains silica and very quickly blunts tools. It also contains oil which inhibits some glues, and surfaces should be washed in methylated spirits before gluing. Teak is one of the outstanding timbers of the world and in recent years has achieved great popularity as a furniture timber. Stiffness II, stability I, hardness I/II.

Utile (Entandophragma utile, West Africa)
Utile resembles sapele but has a less interlocked grain. It works well apart from a tendency to tear when planed and is moderately stable in use. Utile lacks the character of mahogany or sapele and although widely used for high class joinery it cannot be regarded as a top quality furniture wood. Stiffness II, stability II, hardness II.

Walnut, American (Juglans nigra, North America) and Walnut, European (Juglans regia, Europe)
Walnut is a greyish brown wood with irregular dark streaks but the appearance is variable and depends upon its place of origin. There is a large proportion of defective timber so the recovery rate is low and the highly decorative veneers come from the stumps, burrs and forks of a small number of trees. The timber works and finishes well. Stiffness II, stability I, hardness II.

Softwoods
There are many commercial softwoods such as Scots pine, Norway spruce and Silver fir from Europe, Douglas fir, Sitka spruce, Western Hemlock, Lodgepole pine and the Pitch pines from North America and Parana pine from South America. All of these species are suitable for general joinery work or for making painted furniture but there are few softwoods which can be regarded as high quality furniture timbers. There is, at present, a vogue for Scots pine furniture and much antique furniture and fire surrounds which were originally painted are being stripped to reveal what is, quite often, mediocre workmanship. There is, however, one outstanding softwood which behaves like a hardwood. This is yew.

Yew (Taxus baccata, Europe)
When freshly planed yew is a very pale, pinkish-brown wood, often with paler streaks, but it soon mellows to a more uniform pale golden brown. It is fine textured but with a strong contrast between early and late wood. It is possible to select pieces of yew having a very straight grain but much of the grain is irregular. The annual rings and the irregular grain give yew an attractive figure. It is a little difficult to work partly because of the irregular grain and partly because small pieces are liable to flake off the outside of the wood when mortice joints are being cut, otherwise it works well and takes a fine, almost bone-like finish. Due to the irregular growth it splits and checks badly when seasoning and the recovery of sizeable pieces of wood free of defects is very low. When yew has a straight grain it is stable in use. Stiffness I, stability II, hardness I.

Sources of wood
Most of the timbers mentioned above can be bought from timber merchants although yew and walnut may be difficult to obtain in large sizes. However long or carefully the wood has been seasoned it is unlikely, when bought, to have an equilibrium moisture content as low as 12 per cent; it is, therefore, desirable to store it indoors for several months, preferably in a heated room, before using it.

Because new timber is expensive and probably

not fully seasoned it is worthwhile looking for other sources of wood. It is sometimes possible to buy cheaply old furniture containing high quality wood. This, however, is becoming a less likely source as the value of even poor quality and damaged furniture is rising and as late nineteenth or even early twentieth century furniture is coming to be regarded as antique. There are occasionally sales or auctions of timber from the stocks of builders who, for one reason or another, are closing down. Much of the wood used in the furniture illustrated in this book was bought in this way. Good quality softwood is often available from contractors who dismantle old buildings. It is usually full of nails and often painted, but if carefully chosen is suitable for domestic joinery work and costs much less than the normal commercial price in the shop. Painted wood, however, is difficult to work because it blunts and even chips plane blades in a very short time. If such wood is used the paint should be removed by burning, chemical stripping or scraping before planing. It may also be possible for the amateur, provided he is prepared to wait a year or two for the wood, to buy a standing tree and arrange for it to be felled and sawn by a local mill. This is how the wood was obtained for the yew furniture illustrated in this book. The sawn planks were stacked in a stable for at least two years and the rough furniture components were sawn out by hand and stored indoors for another one or two years before being worked.

CHAPTER 2

The choice of tools

The choice of tools

It is unrealistic to be dogmatic about what tools are needed by the amateur. The choice depends upon a number of factors – his experience, his personal preferences, what he proposes to make and how much he is prepared to spend. On the other hand the choice is dictated by technical considerations and the two lists below are a guide, based upon personal experience, to what is necessary for the type of work described in this book. The first list comprises the items thought to be essential while the second comprises those thought to be very useful because they can make the work easier, quicker or more accurate. It is, for example, possible to plane a long edge true with a smoothing or jack plane, but easier and quicker to do it with a fore or jointer plane and for long pieces of wood a long straight edge is obviously better than a short one.

It will be noticed that there are no power tools in either list. This is because they are quite expensive and the drilling, sawing and sanding that can be done with a small electric drill and its attachments can usually be done almost as easily and often better by hand. The larger and very much more expensive machines used by the professionals are a different matter altogether but they are not considered to be within the resources of the average amateur.

In most modern planes the depth of the cut is adjusted with a screw and the lateral alignment with a lever, but it is possible to buy planes in which the blade is adjusted by a process of trial and error. The amateur is strongly advised to choose the screw-adjusted versions because they are likely to save him a considerable amount of time and frustration.

It is always a mistake to buy tools of inferior quality. Steel which will not hold an edge, try squares which are not at 90°, or mitre boxes which do not cut at 45° are more trouble than they are worth. It is also a mistake to buy a made-up tool kit because it will almost certainly contain tools which are not really necessary. Good quality, well chosen tools can be regarded as an investment.

The essential list

(1) Smoothing plane or jack plane
(2) Adjustable block plane
(3) Plough plane
(4) Open-throated router plane
(5) Small router plane
(6) Screw-adjusted round-bottomed spokeshave
(7) Cabinet-maker's scraper
(8) Bevel-edge chisels: 3 mm ($\frac{1}{8}$ in), 6 mm ($\frac{1}{4}$ in), 12 mm ($\frac{1}{2}$ in), 24 mm (1 in). Mortice chisels: 6 mm ($\frac{1}{4}$ in), 10 mm ($\frac{3}{8}$ in). Firmer chisels: 6 mm ($\frac{1}{4}$ in), 12 mm ($\frac{1}{2}$ in), 18 mm ($\frac{3}{4}$ in).
(9) Wooden mallet
(10) Panel saw, about 10 teeth to 25 mm (1 in)
(11) Medium tenon saw, about 14 teeth to 25 mm (1 in)
(12) Dovetail tenon saw, about 20 teeth to 25 mm (1 in)
(13) Coping saw
(14) Keyhole saw
(15) Hand drill
(16) Set of twist drills and countersink drill
(17) Try square
(18) Sliding bevel
(19) Steel straight edge, about 800 mm (30 in)
(20) Flexible steel rule
(21) Marking gauge
(22) Mortice gauge
(23) Marking knife
(24) Bench holdfast
(25) Bench vice
(26) G cramps: about 125 mm (5 in), at least two;
about 62 mm ($2\frac{1}{2}$ in), at least two.
(27) Sash cramps: 950 mm (36 in), two; 1150–1600 mm (48–60 in), four
(28) Screwdrivers, small, medium and large
(29) Flat file for sharpening cabinet-maker's scraper
(30) Rasp
(31) Sharpening stone
(32) Honing guide
(33) Spirit level

(34)   Grinding wheel, hand powered
(35)   Bench
(36)   Bench hook
(37)   Shooting board   } 35 to 40 can
(38)   Winding or parallel boards   be made at
(39)   Mitre template   home
(40)   Mitre box

The non-essential list
(1)   Jack plane or smoothing plane
(2)   Fore or jointer plane
(3)   Spare blade for fore or jointer plane
(4)   Bull-nose plane, 100 mm (4 in)
(5)   Rebate plane, (also known as a rabbet plane)
(6)   Combination plane
(7)   Screw-adjusted flat-bottomed spokeshave

(8)   Bevel-edge chisel 36 mm (1½ in)
(9)   Double-handed scraper
(10)   Steel straight edge, about 1400 mm (54 in), only needed for relatively large-scale work
(11)   Rip saw
(12)   Combination square
(13)   Cutting gauge
(14)   Hand brace
(15)   Twist bits, sizes as required

For particular jobs other tools may have to be bought or made by the worker. It is often worthwhile making a simple jig or template to assist in an operation which has to be repeated a number of times.

sash cramp and lengthening bar

firmer chisel

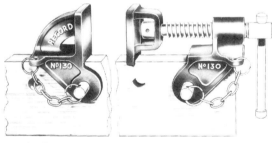

cramp head

mortice chisel

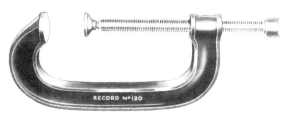

'G' cramp

bevel-edge chisel

9   *Woodworking tools*

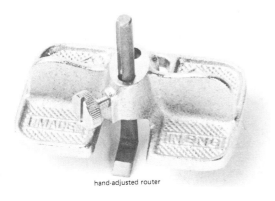

hand-adjusted router

screw-adjusted router

10   Woodworking tools

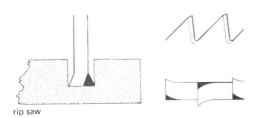

rip saw

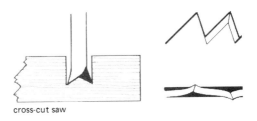

cross-cut saw

combination square

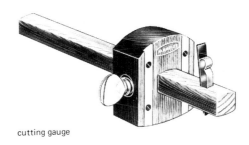

cutting gauge

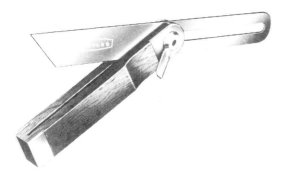

sliding bevel

mortice gauge

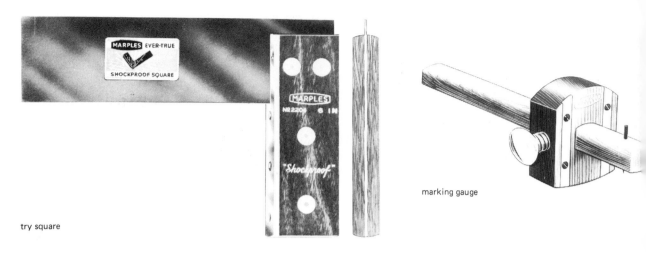

try square

marking gauge

11   Woodworking tools

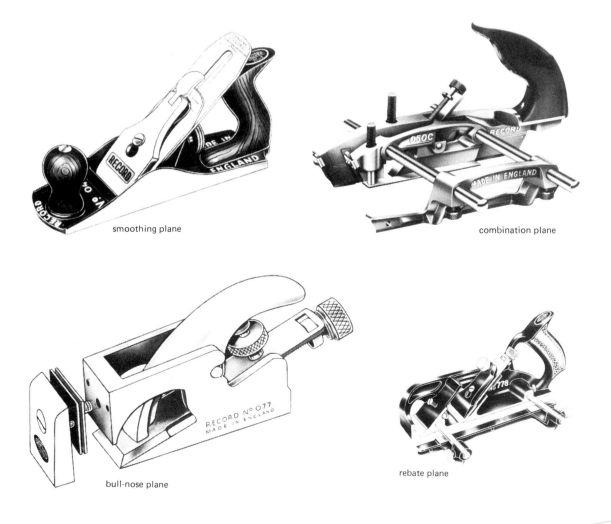

smoothing plane

combination plane

bull-nose plane

rebate plane

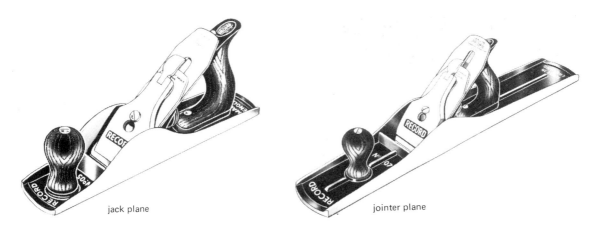

jack plane   jointer plane

screw-adjusted spokeshave

General principles

Tools should always be kept in a warm, dry atmosphere. If they are left in an unheated or badly ventilated workroom or shed they will almost certainly deteriorate. It is also a wise precaution, if tools are not to be used for a time, to wipe them with an oily rag as a precaution against rusting.

Cutting tools are efficient and produce good work only if they are sharp. When working with some species, such as teak, it may be necessary to sharpen a plane blade every few minutes. This is a tedious process and there is always a temptation to delay re-sharpening, but the temptation should be resisted, because in the long run sharp tools not only produce better work but they are also more pleasant, safer and less tiring to use. It is particularly inadvisable to try to finish a piece of work with a blunt tool because the nearer the work comes to completion the more important it becomes to use a sharp tool which produces a clean and accurate finish. But it is not only tools with cutting edges which need to be properly maintained. Nearly all tools require some form of maintenance from time to time.

Truing and smoothing planes
Functions
Truing and smoothing planes perform three functions. These are to cut wood to the correct thickness, to make it true on all sides and edges and to make it smooth.

Ideally, wood is cut to the approximate thickness with a fore plane, brought to its final dimensions with a jack plane and smoothed with a smoothing plane, while edges for jointing are cut with a jointer plane and the ends trued across the grain with a block plane. In practice, three planes are sufficient – a fore or jack plane, a smoothing plane and a block plane, especially if the fore plane has two blades, one ground for heavy cutting and one for jointing. The block plane can also be used for a variety of small trimming and shaping jobs.
Construction
The construction of a plane is shown in figure 12.

To remove the blade the cam is lifted and the lever cap slid upwards and away from the lever-cap screw. The plane blade and the cap iron which are held together by the cap-iron screw are lifted out together. Some cap irons are made in two pieces so that the lower portion lifts off and allows the blade to be sharpened without removing the cap-iron screw. If the cap iron is in one piece, however, it has to be removed by unscrewing the cap-iron screw before the blade can be sharpened. The plane is re-assembled in the reverse order, care being taken when replacing the cap iron not to scrape it against the cutting edge of the blade. The blade has to rest flat on the frog with the top of the

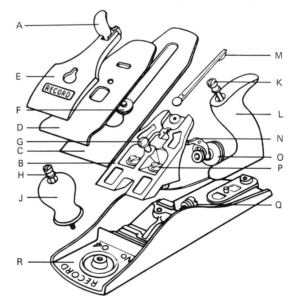

12 *The construction of a smoothing plane*

A	*cam*	K	*nut and screw for*
B	*frog*		*handle*
C	*cutter*	L	*handle*
D	*cap iron*	M	*lateral adjusting lever*
E	*lever cap*	N	*Y-adjusting lever*
F	*cap-iron screw*	O	*cutter-adjusting nut*
G	*lever-cap screw*	P	*frog screw with*
H	*nut and screw for*		*washer*
	knob	Q	*frog-adjusting screw*
J	*knob*	R	*body*

Y-adjusting lever fitting cleanly into the small rectangular aperture in the cap iron. The lever cap is then slid back into position and the cam snapped home. If it is either loose or very tight the lever-cap screw should be adjusted.

The projection of the blade against the sole is controlled by the cutter-adjusting nut and its lateral position by the lateral-adjusting lever, the blade moving in the opposite direction to the lever.

The frog is held in position by two vertical holding screws located on either side of the lever-cap screw and a frog-adjusting screw at the back. The opening in the sole of the plane through which the blade projects (the mouth) can be adjusted by loosening the two vertical holding screws and turning the frog-adjusting screw to move the sole backwards or forwards. When it is in the correct position the two vertical screws are re-tightened.

The knob and handle are held in position by screws which can be tightened if either becomes loose.

The block plane, apart from being very much smaller, differs in three important respects from the ordinary plane. It has no cap iron, the blade is fitted with the bevel uppermost and the width of the throat is controlled by a lever in the front of the plane. The blade is set at a very much flatter angle and the reversed bevel cuts more easily into end-grain wood. It also acts as a form of cap iron in curling back the wood shavings.

Grinding, sharpening and setting

Plane blades are ground to an angle of 25° and sharpened to an angle of 30°. As the blade is progressively re-sharpened the 30° bevel becomes wider and wider and sharpening takes longer and longer each time, as shown in figure 13. The blade has therefore to be re-ground from time to time

and it is a good idea to re-grind the blade before a major planing job is started.

The amateur is advised to use a honing guide, although with practice it is possible to judge the angles sufficiently accurately by eye. Grinding can be done on the coarse side of the oilstone but this takes a very long time and a grinding wheel is almost a necessity. When a blade is being ground or sharpened care must be taken to prevent it becoming too hot and thereby losing its temper. This will not happen on a flat grindstone on which light oil is used only to carry away the fine particles of metal. Provided a grinding wheel is used steadily and the blade is not pressed hard against the stone for long periods no lubrication is required. If, however, the blade does become hot it can be dipped from time to time into water or a light oil can be used on the stone as a lubricant. Before grinding, the cutting edge should be tested with a try square to see whether it is at right angles to the sides of the blade. If it is not the asymmetry should be corrected, as shown in figure 14.

While the blade is being ground on the wheel it should be moved steadily from side to side at a constant angle to the stone to produce an even bevel, the angle of which has to be judged by eye and a process of trial and error. The angle can be checked by fixing the blade into the honing guide at an angle of 25° and grinding it on the oil stone. It will soon be apparent whether the bevel produced on the stone is approximately the same as that produced on the wheel. It is, in any case, worthwhile finishing the grinding on the oil stone because the wheel always produces a slightly irregular as well as a slightly hollow bevel.

The blade is sharpened on the fine side of the stone with the honing guide adjusted to 30°. The guide should be moved from side to side to avoid

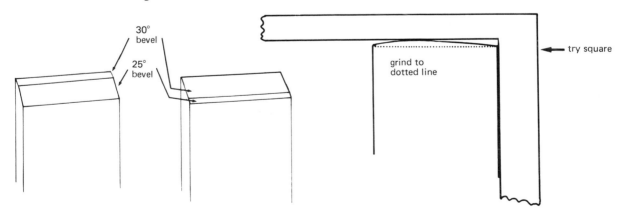

13   *Grinding and sharpening a plane blade*   14   *Testing a plane blade for symmetry*

wearing a groove in the stone, and the sharpening continues until a slight burr can be felt right across the back of the blade on the side without a bevel. When the burr can be felt the blade is reversed and laid perfectly flat upon the stone and rubbed to and fro a few times to remove the burr. It may be necessary to repeat a few strokes on either side before the burr is completely removed. Finally, the edge of the blade is drawn transversely across a piece of hardwood.

There is more than one opinion about the shape of the cutting edge. Some people recommend a completely straight edge with only the extreme corners taken off, while others prefer a slight curve. The author has found a very slight curve to be the most useful shape for smoothing and jointing and a more pronounced curve for planing down to size. This is the reason for recommending two blades for the fore plane which can then be used both for rough, heavy work and for jointing. The block plane blade should be completely straight. These shapes are shown in figure 15.

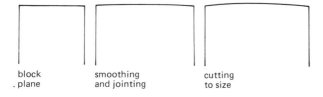

block plane   smoothing and jointing   cutting to size

15   Shapes of cutting edges of plane blades

The position of the cap iron relative to the cutting edge is important. The function of the cap iron is to curl back the shavings and to prevent wood with irregular grain from tearing. As a general rule the cap iron is set back about 1.5 mm (₁/₁₆ in) for rough work and about half that distance for fine work. But the optimum distance is partly determined by the regularity of the grain, the more irregular it is the closer should be the cap iron to the edge of the blade. When the cap iron is set very close to the edge the wood fibres are sometimes forced between the cap iron and the blade. It is immediately apparent when this happens because the plane stops cutting cleanly and feels very woolly. It may also be an indication that the cap iron is not resting perfectly flush on to the back of the blade and therefore needs grinding true.

When the blade has been sharpened and fitted into the plane it has to be adjusted laterally and for depth. In order to do this the plane is held upside down so that the worker can sight along the sole of the plane against a piece of white paper or board,

white surface

16   Adjusting a plane blade

as shown in figure 16. The blade is adjusted until it is just visible as a hairline across and parallel with the sole of the plane. Subsequent adjustments can be made according to the thickness of the shavings produced.

Use

The first requirement is a firm, flat surface on which to plane and an adjustable stop to prevent the wood moving. If the surface is concave the plane will not cut the middle of the wood. If it is convex the wood is liable to ride over the stop. This is shown in figure 17. Even if the bench top is flat, the underside of the wood may be concave, in which case a thin sliver of wood or a steel ruler may be put under the middle of the wood to prevent it bending under the pressure of the plane.

Planing is an arduous activity but there are four ways of reducing the effort. First of all the worker needs to get his weight behind the plane and to work with a rhythm. This is made easier if the wood is not only prevented from moving forwards by the stop but also from moving backwards by a back stop if this can be improvised on the bench. Next the blade should be sharp and the shavings not too thick. Lastly, the sole of the plane should be lubricated by rubbing a candle across it.

At the beginning of each stroke of the plane the main downward pressure should be on the front of the plane and at the end of the stroke on the back of the plane (figure 18). If this is not done the top of the work gradually becomes convex.

If the wood has sloping grain the plane should cut in the direction of the slope to prevent tearing but if the grain is irregular or interlocked this is not possible and the solution is to keep the blade exceptionally sharp, to fit the cap iron very close to the cutting edge, to cut very fine shavings and, with very difficult wood, to reduce the width of the throat by adjusting the position of the frog. It is also sometimes worthwhile planing across the grain, taking care not to plane right to the far edge since this causes the wood to break away. The various methods are illustrated in figure 19.

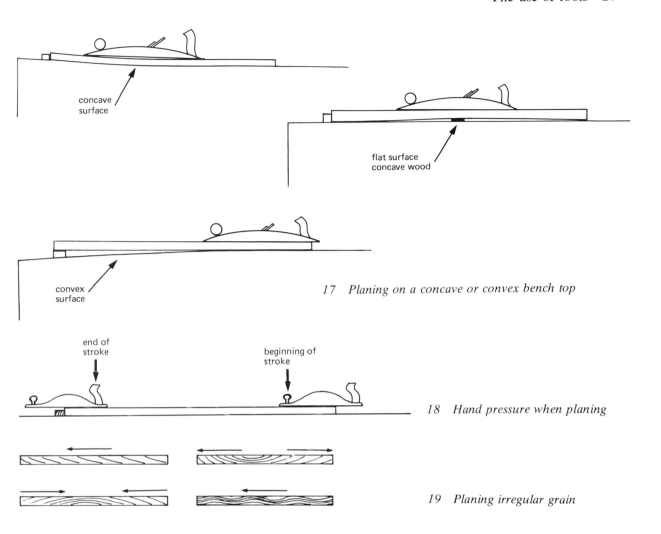

concave
surface

flat surface
concave wood

convex
surface

17   *Planing on a concave or convex bench top*

end of
stroke

beginning of
stroke

18   *Hand pressure when planing*

19   *Planing irregular grain*

Ploughing, rebating and moulding planes
Functions

There are numerous models of ploughing, rebating and combination planes on the market. The simplest form of ploughing plane does not have a fully adjustable blade and takes a range of blades up to about 6 mm ($\frac{1}{4}$ in) wide. It can groove up to about 100 mm (4 in) from the edge of the work and to a depth of about 12 mm ($\frac{1}{2}$ in). It can also be used to cut rebates up to 6 mm ($\frac{1}{4}$ in) wide, as shown in figure 20.

The rebate plane is not designed to cut grooves but it can cut wider rebates – typically up to about 36 mm ($1\frac{1}{2}$ in). It usually has two positions for the blade, one of them being very close to the toe of the plane so that it can be used close up to the end of a stopped rebate. The combination plane is a more elaborate tool which can be used for rebating and grooving to a greater width and to a greater distance from the edge of the wood than a simple plough plane. It can also be used for tonguing and grooving and for working a limited range of mouldings both with and across the grain.

Construction

Detailed descriptions of all these specialized planes are always provided by the manufacturers. They all have in common an adjustable fence which controls the width of the rebate or the distance of the groove from the working edge or face of the wood and an adjustable depth gauge which controls the depth of the grove or rebate. Most of them also have a small sharp spur which can be positioned just in front of the far side of the blade when rebating across the grain. This cuts the wood fibres in front of the blade and prevents the wood from tearing. The essential features are shown in figure 21 which illustrates a simple plough plane.

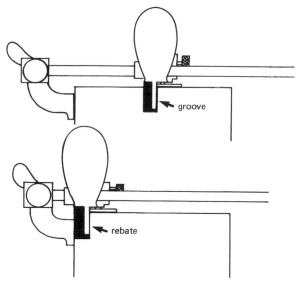

20   *The use of a simple plough plane*

21   *The construction of a simple plough plane*

Grinding, sharpening and setting
The blades are ground and sharpened in exactly the same way as normal plane blades, but the cutting edges have to be perfectly straight and at right angles to the sides of the blades. There is no cap iron to the blade which is held in position by a lever cap and lever-cap screw. For both rebating and grooving the blade should be set so that it projects a hairsbreadth beyond the far side of the body of the plane. If it does not, the rebate or groove is likely to trend towards the near edge of the wood as it becomes deeper. This is illustrated in figure 22.

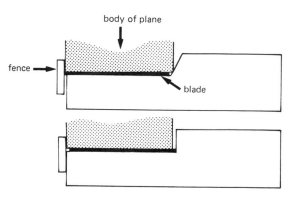

22   *Setting the blade for rebating*

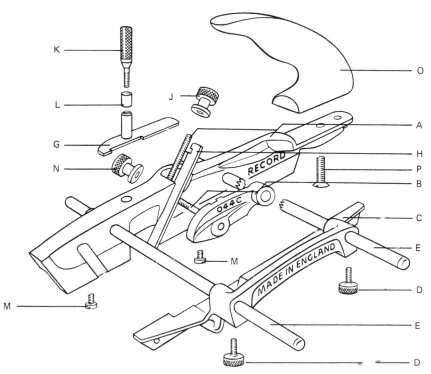

A   *body and cutter adjusting screw*
B   *cutter clamping bracket and cutter clamping screw*
C   *fence*
D   *fence knurled screws (2)*
E   *fence arms (2)*
G   *depth gauge and stem*
H   *cutter*
J   *cutter adjusting nut*
K   *depth gauge locking screw*
L   *depth gauge expander*
M   *fence arm setscrews (2)*
N   *cutter clamping nut*
O   *handle*
P   *handle fixing screw*

Use

The most common ploughing and rebating jobs for the amateur are ploughing grooves for jointing planks edge to edge, grooving the inner edges of door stiles and rails to take panels (page 85), and rebating the backs of carcases to take the back panels. All these jobs can be done with a simple plough plane. Probably the most difficult and important part of the operation is to grind, sharpen and set the blade. If this is done properly little difficulty will be experienced. The blade should always be set to cut thin shavings. The first cuts of a groove or rebate are made at the far end of the work and at each successive cut the plane is brought back a little further until it takes a shaving along the whole length. This, together with a firm inward pressure, helps prevent the plane from drifting outwards towards the worker.

If a groove or rebate has to stop short of the end of the work a sufficient length has to be cut out with a chisel to accommodate that part of the plane which projects beyond the blade.

Router planes

Functions

Router planes are used to clean out grooves of various shapes and to cut them level and to a predetermined depth. They are, therefore, useful for such jobs as preparing the housings for inlays (page 97), hinges (page 126), chessboard squares (page 99) and for truing up tenon joints (page 58).

Construction

The simplest form of router is a home-made tool consisting of two identical pieces of hardwood which are screwed together to hold a thin steel blade and which are shaped into a fence at one end, as shown in figure 23. This router acts as a scraper rather than a cutter and the blade can be adjusted for depth and for the distance from the fence.

A more sophisticated tool is the simple steel router, shown in figure 10. This has to be adjusted by hand and is fitted with only one small blade.

The screw-adjusted router is also shown in figure 10. This is a very useful tool because it can take a range of blades of different shapes and sizes

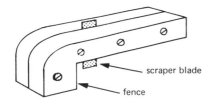

23   A home-made router plane

and being screw-adjusted is more precise and quicker to use. It can also straddle a wider span.

Grinding and sharpening

The blades are sharpened to the usual angles of 25° and 30° but owing to their foot-like shape an ordinary oil stone cannot easily be used. A small hand stone has to be used instead and the stone rubbed against the blade rather than the blade against the stone.

Use

The use of the router depends upon the job to be done. A router is often used to deepen and level a housing cut with a chisel. This involves the progressive lowering of the blade so that on each pass only a thin shaving is removed. There is no difficulty in making fine adjustments to the screw-adjusted type but more care is needed when the tool is hand adjusted. As the holding screw is undone the blade is held firmly in position and then tapped lightly with the screwdriver against the pressure of the fingers to increase its depth very slightly.

Bull-nose plane

Functions

The bull-nose plane has several functions. It can be used as a form of rebate or wide grooving plane to work up close to the ends of housings or stopped grooves or, because the blade extends to the edge of the body, it can be used for various jobs which entail trimming right up an edge or shoulder.

Construction

The bull-nose plane has a small compact body as shown in Figure 11, the front of which can be removed so that the blade projects beyond the front of the tool. The blade is held bevel uppermost, like a block plane, and is adjusted with a screw.

Spokeshave

Function

The flat-bottomed spokeshave is used for cutting convex curves and the round-bottomed spoke-shave for cutting concave curves. They are often used to cut and trim accurately curves which have been cut roughly to shape with a coping saw. Of the two types the round-bottomed version is rather more versatile.

Construction

The depth of cut and the lateral adjustment of the blade of a screw-adjusted spokeshave are controlled by two nuts and the blade is held in position by a lever cap and lever-cap screw. See figure 11.

Grinding, sharpening and setting
The blade is ground and sharpened like any plane blade. There is no cap iron but the projection of the blade below the sole is adjusted in the same way as an ordinary plane with two adjusting nuts. The blade cannot be held in a honing guide because it is too short but it can be held against a wooden block, cut to the correct angles, while it is ground and sharpened on the oilstone, as shown in figure 24.

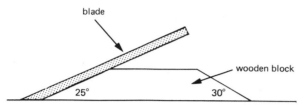

24   *Grinding and sharpening a spokeshave blade*

Use
The spokeshave is always used with the grain to prevent tearing and both the work and the spokeshave have to be held firmly to prevent juddering, which causes ripples to appear on the cut surface of the wood.

Cabinet-maker's scraper
Function
The scraper, which is simply a thin rectangle of steel, is an invaluable tool for producing a fine, smooth surface, particularly on wood with irregular or interlocked grain. It is used after the smoothing plane and before the coarser grade of aluminium oxide paper.

Sharpening
There is a certain knack in sharpening a scraper which has to be learned, and which is illustrated in figure 25. There are five stages in the sharpening process.
1   Clamp the scraper in a vice and carefully file the edge square and flat with a fine, flat file.
2   Remove the scraper from the vice and rub the filed surface on the fine side of the oilstone keeping it perfectly square.
3   With the face of the scraper perfectly flat on the stone rub off the burr first from one edge and then from the other.
4   In order to harden the edge lie the scraper flat on the bench and rub a hard steel tool, such as the back of a gouge, 20 to 30 times along each side. The gouge must lie perfectly flat on the scraper.
5   Clamp the scraper once more in a vice and draw the back of the gouge very firmly along the edge several times, at first at right angles to the blade but finishing at an angle of about 15° from the horizontal. A tool used for turning the edge of a scraper is known as a ticketer.

Use
The scraper can be held in two ways either by pushing the thumbs against the back, when the edge is slightly bowed, or by pulling the scraper with the edge perfectly straight. With either method a properly sharpened scraper should cut

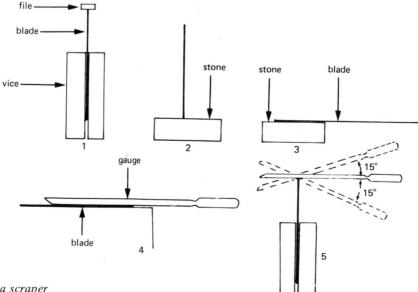

25   *Sharpening a scraper*

very fine, continuous shavings, but it will not keep its edge for long and frequent re-sharpening is necessary. When it is pushed with the thumbs it cuts a little deeper because of the slight bowing but also gets so hot that it is sometimes necessary to wear gloves.

Double-handed scraper
Function
The double-handed scraper performs a similar function to the hand scraper and is particularly useful in cleaning up exposed dovetail joints in such places as drawer sides.
Construction
The double-handed scraper closely resembles a metal spokeshave in construction but it has a scraping instead of a cutting blade.
Grinding, sharpening and setting
Detailed instructions are provided with the tool by the manufacturer. The process of grinding and sharpening is similar to that for a hand scraper except that the blade is bevelled to an angle of 45° instead of 90°.
Use
As with any scraper some practice is required before the tool can be operated to its best advantage. It has to be used with smooth, relatively light strokes and with a fairly fine setting. It is generally more efficient when cutting diagonally to the grain especially when working inwards from the edge of the work.

Chisels
Functions
Chisels are used for paring and slicing and cutting dovetails and mortice-and-tenon joints.
Construction
Bevel-edge chisels, which are used for paring and slicing, have a bevel on all three sides of the blade. This enables them to be used in angles and corners. Firmer chisels which are used for heavy cutting across the grain, as in cutting dovetails, are bevelled only on the cutting edge. Mortice chisels are a specially strengthened type of firmer chisel with a blade which is both long and deep in relation to its width. They often have a leather shock absorber in the handle.
Grinding and sharpening
Chisels are ground and sharpened like plane blades except that firmer chisels used for heavy work on tough wood are better sharpened to an angle of about 35° instead of the usual 30° since this gives more strength and makes the edge less likely to chip.

Use
Chisels are the most dangerous of all hand tools and should never be used with the hands in front of the blade. The edge should always be very sharp and, when paring or slicing, the wood should be removed in very thin shavings and the work held in such a way that it will not move or slip.

If the chisel is being used without a mallet, one hand applies the pressure on the handle and the other guides and steadies the blade. If there is a risk of a chisel cutting too far and damaging the work it is much safer to use a mallet than to apply hand pressure. The force exerted by the mallet is perfectly controllable and immediately dissipated after the blow whereas it takes an appreciable time to release the pressure applied by the hands. Some specialized uses of the chisel are described in more detail in the chapters on joints.

Saws
Functions
The rip saw is used for cutting large pieces of wood in the direction of the grain. It has large teeth and produces a coarse finish. The panel saw is used for cutting across the grain and for general sawing where a finer finish is required. Tenon saws are used for small-scale, precise work. The coping saw is used for cutting curves in relatively small-scale work and the keyhole saw, as its name implies, is used for cutting small holes.
Construction
Rip saws and panel saws are of conventional shape whereas tenon saws have a rectangular blade with a steel or brass backing to give them rigidity. The coping saw is simply a tougher version of the fret saw and has thin, removable blades which can be set in any direction relative to the plane of the saw. The rip saw has chisel-like teeth while all other saws have knife-like teeth, figure 10.

A rip saw has about four teeth to 25 mm (1 in), a panel saw about 10, a general-purpose tenon saw about 14, and a dovetail tenon saw about 20. The usual form of keyhole saw consists of a thin knife-like blade which fits into a trimming-knife handle.
Sharpening and setting
Sharpening and setting are specialized jobs and the amateur is advised to have them done by a professional saw doctor.
Use
Almost all sawn surfaces are subsequently finished with a plane. The saw cut is normally, therefore, not made on the marked line but a little outside it and if the timber is likely to distort as a result of the

saw cut relieving internal stresses in the wood the cut should be made even further from the marked line.

The larger the teeth of the saw the more difficult it is to start the cut accurately and the saw blade should always be steadied for the first few strokes by the thumb. The saw is held with the index finger pointing down the blade and the worker should get his shoulder directly behind the blade and make long steady strokes, concentrating on keeping the saw straight and vertical. If the saw is sharp no particular pressure is required except when ripping long, thick pieces of wood. This is an arduous process and the saw cuts very much more quickly if both hands are used with the left hand pressing the saw against the cut.

If the saw cut should close up and jam the saw, a small wedge or a screwdriver can be pushed in to ease the pressure, and if sawdust obscures the mark it should be brushed away. It is often easier to blow the dust out of the way but this is inadvisable indoors because a dusty atmosphere is unpleasant to work in.

When the cut is almost finished the waste piece of wood has to be supported to prevent it breaking off and perhaps damaging the work. This is particularly important when ripping wood with sloping or irregular grain or when cross cutting. Indeed, when cross cutting it is sometimes advisable to reverse the wood and finish the cut from the other direction.

The work should always be held as firmly as possible while it is being sawn and there are various ways of doing this. For longer cuts made with a panel or rip saw a stout stool or trestle makes a suitable base and for a right-handed worker the wood is held firmly with the left knee and hand. For cuts more than 1m (3 ft) long two supports are often necessary and although wood can always be ripped between two supports it cannot be cross cut because it tends to bend and nip the saw. For smaller and more precise work the bench hook, vice, mitre block or bench holdfast are used. If wood is held in the vice it should not be allowed to project too far because it will tend to judder. If the bench hook or mitre block are used they can themselves be held in the vice for greater stability. If an internal cut is to be made in the centre of a piece of wood a hole is drilled first and the thin blade of the coping saw inserted through the hole and fitted into the saw. This is only possible if the piece of wood is sufficiently small for the frame of the saw to clear the edge of the wood. If it will not, the cut is made with a keyhole saw.

Because the coping saw is used only for curved and often intricate cuts the sawn surface is often finished with a rasp and sandpaper and not with a plane. It therefore saves a great deal of time and effort if the cut is made very close to the line, and this calls for special care in keeping the blade at right angles to the surface of the wood.

Drilling tools
Function
The two drilling tools included in the lists in Chapter 2 are the brace which is used with a range of bits and the hand drill which is used with a range of twist drills. The brace and bit is used for boring larger holes ranging in diameter from about 8 mm ($\frac{5}{16}$ in) to over 25mm (1 in) and it is possible to buy an adjustable bit which will extend to almost 50 mm (2 in). This is designed for softwoods and is not effective when used on hardwoods. Better quality braces have a ratchet action so that they can be used in a confined space without having to be turned through 360°.

The hand drill, which is likely to be used more often in furniture making, drills holes from about 8 mm ($\frac{5}{16}$ in) down to about 1 mm ($\frac{1}{32}$ in). Smaller drills are obtainable or can be made from needles, but they are used for model making rather than for making furniture. Better quality hand drills have two pinions which give a smoother drive.

Various patterns of bits and twist drills are available for specialized purposes but the differences are of litttle significance for normal work.
Use
Whenever possible a hole should not be bored right through a piece of wood from one side because the twist drill and more especially the bit will cause the wood to break away from the far side. As soon as the point of the bit appears on the far side the wood should be turned and the hole finished in the reverse direction. It is often impracticable to avoid some splintering on the far side and this should be removed before the wood is screwed or glued against another surface. This can be done by cutting a very shallow countersink.

The most common use of the twist drill is to prepare holes for screws. At least two sizes of twist drill are required for this. One is to make a hole having the same diameter as the shank of the screw and another one or two to make a hole for the thread, as in figure 184. The hole for the thread should be about the diameter of its solid central core.

Some form of depth gauge is often required

when drilling holes. It is obvious, for example, if the hole for the shank of a screw is drilled too deep that some of the thread will not bite into the wood. Conversely, if the hole is not drilled deeply enough, especially if it is near an edge, the screw is liable to split the wood. Drills are sometimes fitted by the manufacturer with plastic sleeves which can be slid up and down to act as a gauge. A small piece of wood with the appropriate sized hole drilled through it can also be used or, in an emergency, a tiny dab of paint.

The point of a bit can always be located precisely but twist drills, and especially the larger sizes, are liable to wander a little when the hole is started. If it is necessary to locate the hole very precisely this should be done with a sharp spike before the drilling is started, the hole made by the spike acting as a guide for the bit.

Holes are generally, but not always required at right angles to the surface of the wood. It is difficult for the worker to judge whether the brace or drill is at the correct angle and a guide is often useful. One or two try squares balanced beside the drill can be used as a guide but if a slanting hole is needed a special guide or jig may have to be prepared. This consists of a squared piece of wood with a hole of the required size and at the correct angle cut through it. The guide is then cramped onto the work and the hole drilled, or at least started, with the bit or drill through the guide, as in figure 26.

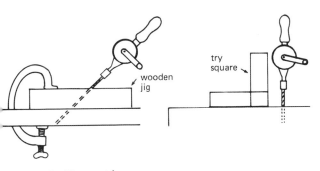

26 Drilling guides

Try square
Function
The try square is used to test right-angled edges for trueness and for marking lines at right angles to the edges or faces of the work.
Construction
The cheaper try squares have a metal blade set in a wooden or plastic stock. The better quality tools are usually made entirely of metal and the most expensive and reliable are engineers' squares

which are designed for metal work. It is important to ensure that a try square is true because many of them, especially the cheaper ones, are not and although woodwork is not an exact science it is disconcerting to find that the diagonals of the top of a cabinet differ by, say, 2 mm (½ in) simply because of an error in the try square.

The amateur is advised to buy a good quality, large woodworking try square plus a small engineer's square. The small tool is useful for small-scale work and can also be used as a reliable criterion of accuracy. A try square should be treated very carefully because a hard knock or a fall can put it out of true.

Combination square
The combination square is, basically, a metal try square in which the stock can slide along the blade and be locked in any position. The blade is marked in imperial or metric units and there is a small spirit level in the stock. The tool can be used for many purposes such as measuring a distance and transferring it directly onto another piece of wood. It also has a particular value in the construction of fitted furniture.

Sliding bevel
Function
The sliding bevel is used for testing or marking an angle.
Construction
The tool is essentially a try square with an adjustable, hinged blade which is usually tightened with a hand nut or lever but sometimes with a screw.

Straight edge
Function
The straight edge is used for testing the straightness and trueness of wood and for marking straight lines.
Construction
The worker is often recommended to make his own wooden straight edge but the author recommends the use of a steel straight edge, in fact two steel straight edges – a shorter and a longer one. The reason for this is that the accuracy of any piece of work depends upon the accuracy of the straight edge and wood is never entirely reliable for the reasons discussed in Chapter 1. Furthermore, it is not practicable to cut deep, marking lines with a trimming knife against a wooden straight edge without the risk of damaging it and yet such marks often need to be made.

Flexible steel rule
The flexible steel rule is used to measure and to mark off distances. Almost any type is suitable.

Marking gauges
Function
There are three different types of gauge, each with a special function. The normal marking gauge has a sharp point for marking lines along the grain parallel with and at a predetermined distance from the edge of the wood. The cutting gauge, which marks with a small blade instead of a point, is used for marking across the grain and also for shallow cutting. The mortice gauge is used for marking mortice-and-tenon joints.
Construction
The construction of all three gauges is very similar. The blade of the cutting gauge is held in position with a small hardwood wedge which allows the blade to be easily removed and reversed so that the flat edge of the blade is against the work, as shown in figure 27.
The mortice gauge has two points which are adjustable with a hand screw to the exact width of the mortice chisel (figure 10).
Use
The only thing to watch when using a gauge is to keep the fence firmly and flat against the edge of the wood, as in figure 27.

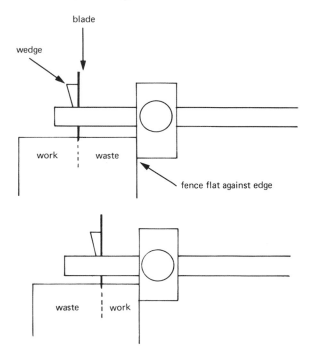

27   *Using a cutting gauge*

Marking knife
The marking knife is used primarily for marking lines, usually against a straight edge or try square. Any sharp, thin bladed knife is suitable for this purpose but the most convenient is probably a small trimming knife with exchangeable blades.

Bench holdfast
Function
The bench holdfast acts as an extra, very strong hand and holds work firmly in position flat on the bench (page 76).
Use
The hole for the holdfast should be about 50–75 mm (2–3 in) deep. Since this is thicker than the average bench top it is usually necessary to fix an additional piece of wood below the top before making the holes for the holdfast, as in figure 28. The holdfast is sometimes supplied with a metal collar which is countersunk into the bench and which acts as a liner to the hole. When fitted with a collar the hole is bored vertically into the bench top. Holes can be bored in two or three convenient positions and a horizontal hole in the right-hand leg allows the holdfast to be used as an auxiliary vice.

Bench vice
The bench vice is discussed in Chapter 8.

Cramps
Function
There are many types of cramp and they have many functions, all of which involve holding two or more pieces of wood firmly together. They can, however, be subdivided into two broad groups – sash cramps which are used almost exclusively for gluing and smaller 'G' type cramps which are used for both gluing and holding. Sash cramps are expensive but an economy can be made by using cramp heads which are fixed to 25 mm (1 in) thick strips of wood in place of the steel bars of the complete cramps. The use of cramps for gluing is discussed in Chapter 16. The smaller G cramps, hand screws, thumb screws and rack cramps are useful for a variety of purposes and it is worthwhile accumulating a small collection of various sizes.

Files and rasps
Files are used in furniture making primarily for sharpening scraper blades but occasionally for shaping wood. Rasps are used for shaping and trimming small diameter curves which are too small for the spokeshave.

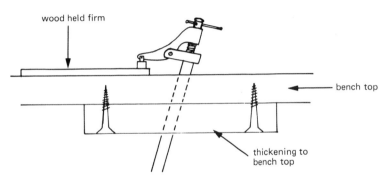

28   *Fixing a bench holdfast*

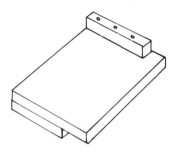

29   *A bench hook*

Spirit level
A spirit level is used in levelling and truing fitted furniture, in levelling sash cramps prior to gluing and in testing boards for twist (page 103).

Bench hook
A bench hook, which is invariably home-made and measures about 200 mm by 250 mm (8 in by 10 in), is used for holding small pieces of wood firmly while they are being cross cut. It consists of three pieces of hardwood put together as shown in figure 29. It is convenient to have, in addition, a small square of wood of the same thickness as the base of the bench hook to support the ends of longer pieces of wood while they are being cut. After some use the bench hook becomes grooved and the underside of the saw cut tends to break away. When this happens it should be re-made.

Shooting board
Function
A shooting board is used for planing the edges of wood straight and square and for truing mitres.
Construction
A shooting board consists of a perfectly flat, stable board usually about 1 m by 250 mm (36 in by 10 in) with a platform along one side and a stop at the end of the platform. The stop is either at right angles for normal work or at 45° for truing mitres. The height of the platform is such that a piece of wood lying on it is about half the width of the plane sole above the base. A shooting board, which is always home-made, is shown in figure 30.
Use
The piece of wood to be trued is held firmly in position against the stop with the edge to be planed parallel with and just overlapping the edge of the platform. The plane is placed on its side on the base and the edge planed in the normal way. The

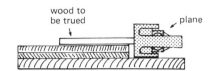

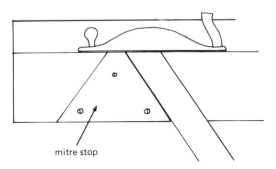

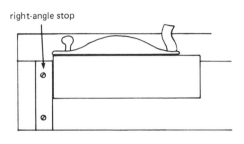

30   *A shooting board*

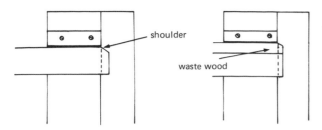

31   *Planing end grain on a shooting board*

plane blade should be set fine and if a long, general purpose plane, such as a fore plane, is used it is worthwhile using a special blade with little or no curve on the cutting edge (page 26) so that it gives a cut exactly at right angles to the base. If end grain is planed the far edge will break away unless an angle is cut down to the mark with a chisel or a piece of waste wood used to support the far edge, as in figure 31.

It is self-evident that the edge produced on a shooting board will not be a true right angle unless the plane blade is straight and parallel with the sole of the plane, the sole of the plane is at right angles to the side of the plane and the shooting board itself is perfectly true. In practice, the edge produced on a shooting board is not always true but it is said that this does not greatly matter if two pieces of wood to be jointed edge to edge are reversed after planing so that the inaccuracies cancel each other out, as in figure 32.

32   *Cancelling inaccuracies in edging*

It is, however, not particularly difficult to plane perfectly true edges without a shooting board and it has been the author's experience that the shooting board is only an advantage when planing very thin pieces of wood. For very small-scale work it may be worth making a small shooting board for use with a block plane.

Mitre box
Function
A mitre box is used to guide the saw when cutting mitres or cross-cutting at right angles to the face edge.
Construction
A mitre box can be bought from a tool shop but the cheaper, wooden ones are often inaccurate and do not provide a guide for cutting at 90° while the metal ones are quite expensive. It is, therefore, better to make one at home because this not only saves money but also gives good practice in accurate planing, marking and sawing. The construction is quite simple and involves cutting three small pieces of wood perfectly true. One piece, which forms the base, is about 300 mm by 90 mm by 50 mm (12 in by 3½ in by 2 in) and the two other pieces which form the sides are about 300 mm by 90 mm by 25 mm (12 in by 3½ by 1 in). The two side pieces are screwed to the base so that their top edges are perfectly parallel and their bottom edges parallel with and about 12 mm (½ in) above the bottom of the base. This allows the box to be fitted easily into a vice. This is shown in figure 33.

After the box has been screwed together 45° and 90° slots are marked out carefully with a protractor and try square, and then cut equally carefully with a tenon saw.
Use
The box is held in a vice and the wood to be mitred or cross cut is held firmly in the box with the face edge against one of the sides while it is cut with a tenon saw. After a period of use the lower parts of the slots become wider due to the action of the saw teeth, and the sides of the box have to be replaced.

Winding strips
Winding strips ('winding' pronounced as in 'binding') are used to test whether a piece of wood is twisted. They comprise two identical strips of wood each about 300 mm by 50 mm by 6 mm (12 in by 2 in by ¼ in). Each strip of wood has parallel sides and is tapered towards one long edge. One strip is painted matt white and one matt black. They are placed across the board to be tested, one at each end and parallel with one another. By standing several feet away it is possible to see if the top edges of the strips indicate any twist in the wood. See figure 34

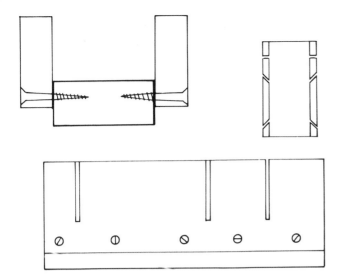

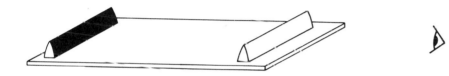

33   A home-made mitre box

34   The use of winding strips

A piece of furniture should, above all, perform the functions required of it. It should be sufficiently strong and robust for its purpose and should be so designed that it is not distorted or damaged by the inevitable movement of the wood with changes in humidity. Its construction should be within the competence of the craftsman and it should be pleasing to the eye. There are, therefore, two broad factors to be taken into account; the one technical and the other aesthetic, the relative importance of which depends upon the intended purpose. At the one extreme, some furniture is almost entirely utilitarian and its design is strongly influenced by technical considerations. At the other extreme the prime object may be to create something of beauty and craftsmanship. But if either purpose completely dominates so that the furniture has either utility without beauty or beauty without utility then the design cannot be good. Indeed, furniture without utility ceases to be furniture and becomes mere decoration.

The technical factors
Fitness for purpose
There is not a great deal to be said about fitness for purpose because it is mainly a matter of commonsense. A bookcase, for example, has to fit into the space available for it and the shelves have to be of a suitable depth and width for the books which it will hold. They must also have sufficient stiffness to take the weight of the books without bending and, bearing in mind the relationship between span and stiffness, this may most effectively and economically be achieved by providing intermediate support in the form of vertical divisions. Stiffness is an important consideration in any piece of furniture having a wide unsupported span, such as a long table or sideboard. If the furniture is likely to be subjected to wide variations in humidity a stable timber is essential and hardness as well as strength is necessary if it is to withstand rough usage.
Allowance for movement
Because all wood shrinks and swells with changes in moisture content furniture has to be made so that it can move without distortion or damage.

There are two ways of doing this. First, a component which will move tangentially or radially to the direction of the grain is not fixed rigidly to a component which will move longitudinally. Secondly, because longitudinal shrinkage is very small, the main structure of any piece of furniture is constructed of longitudinal members. These two principles may be illustrated by considering a cabinet door, the framework of which consists of two vertical stiles and two horizontal rails, all cut longitudinally to the grain. The door will therefore move very little in either a horizontal or vertical direction and what little movement there is will be matched by the carcase itself, which is also made of longitudinal members. The panel of the door, however, has to be free to move tangentially or radially and cannot be fixed rigidly to the frame. It is slotted into grooves or rebates cut into the inner edges of the stiles and rails (page 85) and these grooves or rebates hold it firmly but not rigidly in position. This is illustrated in figure 35 which shows the effect of a change in moisture content on a door with a freely moving panel and on one with a fixed panel.

If a door were not framed but made of one piece of wood it would be liable to shrink within its aperture, as illustrated in figure 36.

A table top is another example of a large sheet of wood free to move tangentially or radially and which is fitted to a frame made of longitudinal members. If the table top were screwed onto the rails of the frame it would be liable to split if the moisture content of the wood were to change. For this reason it is fixed to the rails with wooden buttons which are free to move in small grooves thus allowing the top to move independently of the frame.
The experience of the craftsman
Technical skill develops with practice and most amateurs gain their initial experience in the handling of tools and the use of wood by doing relatively simple jobs in the house such as putting up shelves or making fitted cupboards. The development of an ability to do finer work depends upon the acquisition of technical skill. An amateur can never acquire the dexterity and assurance of a

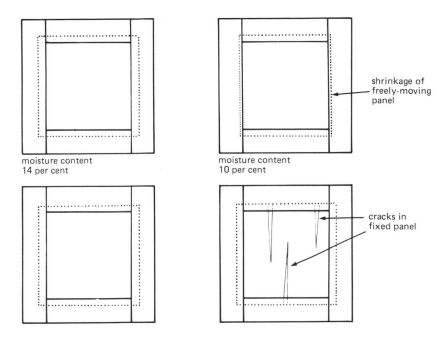

moisture content
14 per cent

moisture content
10 per cent

shrinkage of
freely-moving
panel

cracks in
fixed panel

35   *The effect of shrinkage on a door panel*

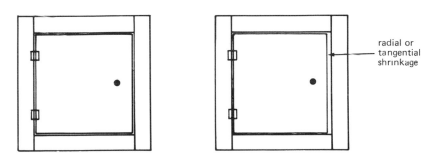

radial or
tangential
shrinkage

36   *The effect of shrinkage on a solid door*

professional because he cannot devote sufficient time to his work. He has, therefore, to be prepared to make up for his lack of training and experience with a great deal of care and patience. If he is prepared to do this he will succeed in making good quality furniture. If he is not he will be wasting his time.

The process of self training should be productive as well as educational and the worker can make useful articles of furniture in the process of acquiring his skills. Probably the most useful exercise is to make a table. This involves the basic skills of planing wood true and square, of jointing planks edge to edge and of cutting mortice-and-tenon joints. Little can be achieved without these skills and the sooner they are mastered the better. The worker should not be disheartened if his early attempts are less than perfect. Neither should he be discouraged from attempting increasingly challenging tasks, because this develops not only skill but confidence and interest.

The aesthetic factor
There are no absolute criteria of good or bad design. We are all influenced consciously and subconsciously by contemporary fashion and our taste changes with age and experience. It is probable and logical that younger people are more influenced by fashion and older people by their experience. Few amateur furniture makers are trained in design and a practical way of developing ideas is to study the types of furniture which one finds pleasing, not necessarily with the idea of

copying them but rather to allow impressions to develop in one's mind. It will soon become apparent that some of the techniques used in factory-made furniture and some of the skills and methods used by professional craftsmen over the last 300 years cannot be adopted directly by the amateur working, generally, with simple hand tools. It is necessary to adapt and simplify.

The pieces of furniture discussed below reflect the developing competence and the changing taste of the author who makes no claim to skill in design and who has relied to a greater or lesser extent upon the impressions derived from both modern and antique furniture. They also represent the sort of work that any reasonably competent amateur can do if he is prepared to make an effort over a period of time.

The first three items of teak furniture are some of the early pieces made by the author. They are all simple and sturdy in construction, and were useful exercises in planing true, and in cutting mortice-and-tenon and dovetail joints.

The bookcase illustrated in figure 37 has a design fault because the right-hand shelves were made tall enough for large books but are not deep

enough to hold them without overlapping. This fault was corrected in the larger bookcase shown in figure 38 in which the lower shelves are not only taller but also deeper.

The teak table illustrated in figure 39 has iroko legs. It is suitable as a sturdy kitchen or work table. The sideboard shown in figure 40, a more ambitious piece of work, is also made of teak. The slight variation in the colour of the wood is due to the fact that it was made from a mixed batch of secondhand teak bought at an auction. The sideboard relies for its stiffness purely upon the flat planks of the top and bottom of the carcase. As these are of thick teak there is adequate stiffness, but some form of plinth could also have been used.

The chess table shown in figure 41 is made of rosewood and yew. The trolley illustrated in figure 42 is made of secondhand Honduras or Cuban mahogany inlaid with yew chess squares. The design was not consciously derived from any other furniture but is, apart from the chess squares, purely utilitarian. It is a very practical design being completely rigid, easy to push and having large, easily removable trays. Nearly all the furniture illustrated in this book has a plain wax finish but

37   Teak bookcase

38   Teak bookcase

39   Teak and iroko table

40 Teak sideboard

41 Yew and rosewood chess table

42   Mahogany and yew tea trolley

the trolley was given several coats of polyurethane lacquer and then rubbed with fine wire wool to give a reasonably natural finish which is resistant to heat and liquids. The brass sleeves on the legs prevent the thick metal pins of the wheels from splitting the wood.

The painted bookcase and cupboards shown in figure 43 are an example of straightforward utilitarian joinery rather than of cabinet making. The unit is made of whitewood (spruce).

The author was fortunate some years ago in buying a very large yew tree from which it was possible to find sufficient wood to make five sizable pieces of furniture, three of which are illustrated here. The cabinet shown in figure 44 was designed to hold records in the cupboards and other associated equipment, such as headphones and tapes, in the drawer. The drawer and inside edges of the stiles and rails of the door are cock beaded and the plinth is made of hand-cut yew veneer on oak.

The chest of drawers shown in figure 45 obviously owes much of its design to the military chests of the late eighteenth and nineteenth centuries. The chest was made to exploit some very fine and unusually straight-grained planks of yew almost entirely free from defects. The chest, including the drawer sides, is unusual in that it is made entirely of solid yew.

Earlier in this chapter the point was made that furniture may be almost entirely utilitarian or almost entirely decorative but that neither function should entirely dominate the other. All the pieces described above are rather more functional than decorative but the two pieces discussed next were designed to be more decorative than functional.

Figure 46 illustrates a small occasional table. It is made of yew which is cross-banded on the top and sides and inlaid with mahogany. Although influenced by eighteenth century design the table is obviously modern. It took a considerable time to make because the drawer and the three rails are made of handcut veneer on mahogany. It is a

43   *Painted softwood cupboards and bookcase*

1 Yew table inlaid with mahogany

2 Teak sideboard

3 African mahogany D table inlaid with yew, with yew and rosewood chess box

4 Mahogany and yew tea trolley, with inlaid chess board

44 Yew record cabinet

particularly delicate job to cut and glue hand-cut cross banding because it is thin enough to be fragile but thick enough for the edges and mitres to have to be planed true.

The size and shape of the chess box shown in figure 47 were entirely determined by the space needed to accommodate a set of chess-men. It is made of mahogany and veneered with hand-cut yew and rosewood. The design on the lid is intended to suggest a chess board and the rosewood stringing is partly decorative but is partly a device to fill in the gaps left along all the edges by the relatively thick yew veneers.

The last two pieces shown in figures 48 and 49 can be regarded as modern, simplified interpretations of an eighteenth century style. They each show a balance between utility and ornament and they were designed to exploit the very unusual figure on a piece of African mahogany which was found lying in the open in a dirty condition in a builder's yard. The drawer fronts and the curved rails of the D table are made of hand-cut veneer glued onto a base cut from offcuts of utile.

45 *Yew chest of drawers*

46 *Yew table inlaid with mahogany*

47   Yew and rosewood chess box

48   African mahogany D table inlaid with yew

49   African mahogany bow-fronted chest of drawers

Plans and drawings

A professional cabinet maker obviously has to make detailed plans if he is working on a piece of furniture commissioned by a customer and if he intends to make more than one piece of the same design. But for the amateur working for himself detailed plans are not necessary. They are largely a matter of personal preference particularly since he is likely to be making relatively simple furniture. None of the pieces of furniture shown in this book, for example, was made from detailed plans. The author sometimes works from very rough sketches and sometimes from rather more careful drawings although these are rarely followed precisely. The final dimensions and details are decided by observation and by trial and error as the work proceeds. The sketches are, however, sufficiently accurate to allow cutting lists of the various components to be prepared. As an example, the only plan of the bow-fronted chest of drawers shown in figure 49 is reproduced in figure 50.

If one is uncertain about a detail it is sometimes useful to look at other similar pieces of furniture. For example, the precise degree of taper on the legs of the D table illustrated in figure 48 was determined after measuring the size and taper of the legs of several antique tables. For someone without design training it is often easier to visualise

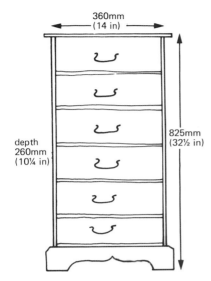

360mm
(14 in)

depth
260mm
(10¼ in)

825mm
(32½ in)

50   Plan of bow-fronted chest of drawers

the most pleasing proportions of a carcase not
from a drawing but either by manipulating the top
and sides before they have finally been cut to
length or by examining other similar pieces of
furniture.

When doing something for the first time it is
sometimes useful to make rough sketches of the
various details of construction although these are
often more easily worked out three dimensionally
on the work itself.

It is necessary to prepare carefully dimensioned
drawings and to follow then closely when making
furniture which is to be fitted permanently into a
confined space in the house because there is no
possibility of changing the overall dimensions as
the work proceeds. The plan for the fitted shelves
and cupboards shown in figure 43 is reproduced
below in figure 51 together with a cutting list and
some aide-memoires.

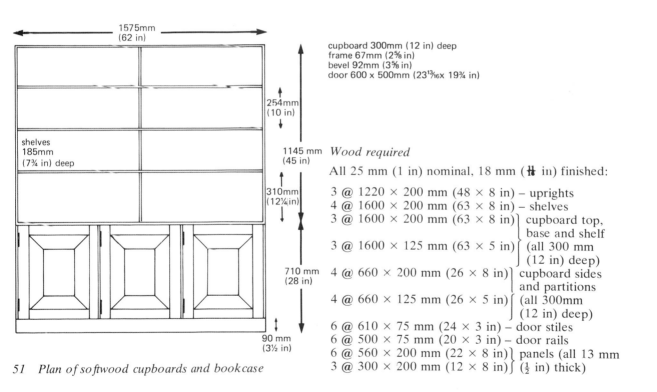

1575mm
(62 in)

254mm
(10 in)

shelves
185mm
(7¾ in) deep

1145 mm
(45 in)

310mm
(12¼ in)

710 mm
(28 in)

90 mm
(3½ in)

51   Plan of softwood cupboards and bookcase

cupboard 300mm (12 in) deep
frame 67mm (2⅝ in)
bevel 92mm (3⅝ in)
door 600 x 500mm (23¹³/₁₆x 19¾ in)

Wood required

All 25 mm (1 in) nominal, 18 mm (⅜ in) finished:

3 @ 1220 × 200 mm (48 × 8 in) – uprights
4 @ 1600 × 200 mm (63 × 8 in) – shelves
3 @ 1600 × 200 mm (63 × 8 in)⎫ cupboard top,
                             ⎪ base and shelf
3 @ 1600 × 125 mm (63 × 5 in)⎬ (all 300 mm
                             ⎪ (12 in) deep)
                             ⎭
4 @ 660 × 200 mm (26 × 8 in)⎫ cupboard sides
                            ⎪ and partitions
4 @ 660 × 125 mm (26 × 5 in)⎬ (all 300mm
                            ⎪ (12 in) deep)
                            ⎭
6 @ 610 × 75 mm (24 × 3 in) – door stiles
6 @ 500 × 75 mm (20 × 3 in) – door rails
6 @ 560 × 200 mm (22 × 8 in)⎫ panels (all 13 mm
3 @ 300 × 200 mm (12 × 8 in)⎭ (½ in) thick)

CHAPTER 5

Cutting, planing and jointing to size

The first stages in making a piece of furniture are to cut out the various components to their approximate sizes and then to plane them true and square to their precise dimensions. Whatever may be the final shape of a component it is necessary, first, to cut and true a rectangular block from which it will be cut. This is illustrated in figure 52.

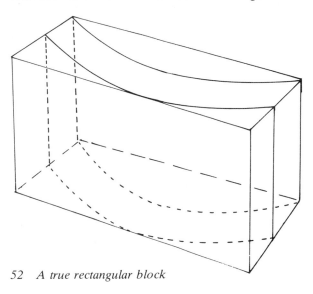

52   *A true rectangular block*

If there are two or more components of the same dimensions the first one to be marked is used as a template to mark the others.

For larger pieces of furniture it is almost always necessary to glue two or more pieces of wood edge to edge to obtain the necessary width.

Cutting to approximate size

If the wood is bought from a timber merchant it is unlikely to be either perfectly flat or to have a moisture content as low as 12 per cent. Some allowance for thickness has, therefore, to be made to allow for truing after it has been fully seasoned. For example, to produce a board 1300 mm by 300 mm by 22 mm (50 in by 12 in by $\frac{7}{8}$ in) from wood which has been stored in an open warehouse it is not unlikely that an initial thickness of about 28 mm ($1\frac{1}{8}$ in) will be required. For smaller dimensions a smaller margin will be adequate.

Wood from other sources may be very much thicker than required and the alternatives are either to do some very arduous ripping with a hand saw or to find an accommodating saw miller or timber merchant whom one can pay to slice it. It is not easy to rip very short lengths on a power saw so the wood should not be cross cut into shorter lengths before it is sliced.

A more common situation is that the wood is a good deal thicker than required but not thick enough to slice with a saw. There is then no alternative but to reduce its thickness with a plane, preferably a fore plane or jack plane with the blade ground into a slight curve (figure 15). If this has to be done each component is first sawn to its approximate length and width before planing. After rough planing to an approximate thickness, when the opportunity should be taken of correcting any significant distortion, the wood should be left for some time in a warm, dry atmosphere, preferably for at least several weeks, before being planed to its final dimensions. During this final phase of seasoning, it is preferable to hold the wood so that its movement is restrained, as shown in figure 53.

53   *Final seasoning of roughly-dimensioned furniture components*

Planing to final dimensions
Sequence of planing
The sequence is first to plane one face flat and true – the face side – and then to plane one longitudinal edge – the face edge – straight and at right angles to it. These two faces are marked with a pencil, as shown in figure 54, and used as reference planes from which the other three edges and the other face are tested for trueness. All measurements are taken and all joints marked from these two faces. If the piece of wood is not to be glued edge to edge the next step is to plane the wood to its final thickness, but if it is to be glued it is better to leave this until after the gluing, because the face sides are then likely to need a little re-truing. After the wood has been planed to its

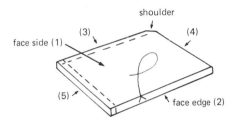

54   Sequence of planing

final thickness it is standard practice to true the two ends and finally the remaining longitudinal edge. The reason for this sequence is to leave some support for the end grain, as shown in figure 54 where the longitudinal edge has been cut back to the mark with a chisel to form a shoulder. The author, however, prefers to true up the second longitudinal edge before the sides. This means that the ends have to be planed from each side towards the middle to avoid splitting the end grain but it does give a precise mark on the longitudinal edge, and not at some distance from it, for planing the end grain. There is, however, little to choose between the two sequences.
The face side
The better side is chosen as the face side because it is usually the external side in the finished work. If the face side is concave longitudinally (bowed) it may be necessary, first, to remove the convexity from the reverse side, so that the wood does not ride over the bench stop. If, on the other hand, the reverse side is concave it may be necessary to put a sliver of wood under it to enable the plane to cut on the face side (figure 17).

It is possible for a piece of wood, when tested with a straight edge, to appear perfectly flat both longitudinally and transversely but to be twisted. The first thing, therefore, is to test for twist (wind) either by testing diagonally with the straight edge or by checking each end with a spirit level, as in figure 55. If the wood is seriously twisted it should be rejected, but there is often a certain amount of twist and it is useful to check at this stage that there will be sufficient thickness left after the wood has been planed flat. It is possible to put a lot of effort into truing the face side only to find at the end that the wood is too thin. If the wood is twisted, as in figure 55, the first thing to do is to remove the high portions at A and D and then to plane in the middle to remove the convexity between B and C, as in figure 56.

When the wind has been roughly removed the wood is tested with the straight edge between E and F, G and H, and I and J, and planed level in the longitudinal plane. It is then tested between K and L, M and N, O and P, and so on, and planed level in

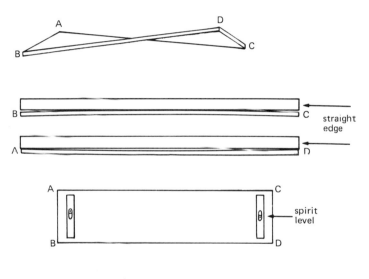

55   Testing for wind

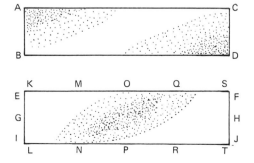

56   Correcting wind

the transverse plane. It is then tested again for wind and any remaining distortion corrected. When the wood has been planed approximately true, the final truing is done with a smoothing plane with the cutter set fine. Particularly difficult areas of irregular grain can sometimes be planed without tearing by working at right angles to the grain.

In the later stages of truing a side, a spirit level is not sufficiently sensitive for testing wind. This is better done by testing the diagonals with a straight edge, or, most precisely, by using winding strips (figure 34).

The face edge

The use of the shooting board (page 35) is a matter of personal preference and experience but the author has found it easier to plane wood more than about 9 mm ($\frac{3}{8}$ in) thick in the vice rather than on the shooting board.

It is not possible to plane an edge true unless the wood is held very firmly. If it is held in the vice, as in figure 57a, it is liable to rock as the pressure of the plane is transferred from one end to the other. This is particularly likely to happen at this stage because the reverse side has not yet been planed

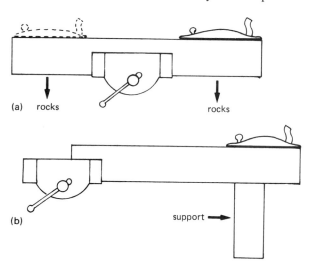

57   *Supporting wood for planing the edge*

flat and parallel with the face side. The difficulty can be overcome by holding the far end of the wood in the vice and supporting the near end, as in figure 57b.

The edge has to be trued in two planes and this is best done with a jointer or fore plane, although it can, with care, be done with a jack plane or smoothing plane. Before planing, the edge is tested for squareness at several points along its length with a try square, and for straightness with a straight edge, so that one has a mental picture of its configuration. First of all the edge is roughly straightened, then squared and finally made perfectly straight, but there are usually, in practice, some successive approximations to be made to both squareness and straightness.

The plane is held as horizontally as possible and supported with the fingers of the left hand which bear against the side of the work. Unless the grain is sloping in the wrong direction the fingers bear against the face side which is smooth. Sometimes, however, to avoid planing against the grain the fingers have to bear against the reverse, rougher side of the work.

The plane is not tilted to remove wood from one side of the edge or the other but instead is moved sideways, as shown in figure 58, where the plane is moved to the right to remove the high side at A and to the left to remove the high side at B.

Frequent testing with the try square and straight edge is necessary to achieve a perfectly true edge. The final cut should take a thin continuous shaving along the entire length of the wood to remove any slight residual irregularities.

The reverse side

The thickness is gauged from the face side with a marking or cutting gauge. If a cutting gauge is used the cutter has to be set as in figure 27b. The method of planing is the same as that described for the face side except that care has to be taken to avoid damaging the surface of the face side. The surface of the bench should be brushed clean and if it is rough it may be advisable to rest the face side on several sheets of newspaper.

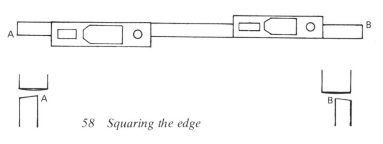

58   *Squaring the edge*

The ends

The right hand end is marked first leaving as little waste as possible to minimize the amount of planing to be done. When the right hand end has been marked the length is measured from it and the left hand end marked in the same way, and the diagonals checked to ensure that the work is perfectly rectangular. The surplus wood is then sawn off to within about 2 mm (🔺 in) of the left-hand mark.

The ends are marked with a marking knife against the blade of a try square. The first mark is made at right angles across the face edge, with the stock of the try square held firmly on the face side. The face side and the reverse side are then both marked from the face edge, never from the reverse edge. Finally, with the stock of the try square on the face side, a mark is made at right angles across the reverse edge to coincide with the transverse marks on the face and reverse sides. If this mark does not exactly coincide with the two transverse marks the work cannot be true. The error is almost certainly on the face side causing the marks on each edge to be not exactly parallel with each other. If the face edge is untrue it affects both transverse marks equally and no discrepancy appears in the marking on the reverse edge.

59   *Inaccurate marking with a try square*

Since the stock of the try square covers only a part of the face edge of a long piece of wood the transverse marks at either end of the work will not be exactly parallel if there is any error in the face edge. This is shown in an exaggerated form in figure 59, and may produce a significant error in a large piece of wood. When accuracy is critical it is possible to avoid the risk of error by taking the right angles from a steel straight edge held against the edge and not from the face edge itself, as in figure 60.

The blade of the try square may not be long enough to reach right across the work, especially if it is separated from the face edge by the width of a straight edge and it is difficult to extend the mark accurately with a straight edge after the try square has been removed. A more reliable method is to hold a steel straight edge firmly against the try square blade, as in figure 60, and to make the entire mark along the straight edge. This introduces a further problem because a long straight edge is difficult to hold firmly with the hand while a mark is being cut against it. It may be necessary, therefore, to hold the far end of the straight edge with a small cramp while making the mark.

The ends can be planed with a smoothing plane but a block plane is better. Care has to be taken to avoid splitting the end grain (figure 61a). The normal method is to plane from each side towards the middle (figure 61b), but this is difficult with very narrow pieces of wood and impossible on a shooting board. There are two solutions to the problem. One is to chisel a shoulder on one edge and to plane against the shoulder, the other is to cramp a piece of waste wood against the edge to protect it (figure 31). On the shooting board a

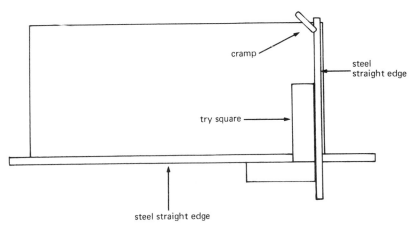

cramp

steel straight edge

try square

steel straight edge

60   *Accurate marking with a try square*

cramp is not necessary because the waste wood is held in position by hand pressure. Frequent testing with the try square is necessary to check that the end is square with the face side and at right angles to the face edge. If the edge was marked with a straight edge, as shown in figure 60, the final testing should be done in the same way. There is frequent mention in this book of the need for a sharp and finely set plane but this is especially important when planing across the grain.

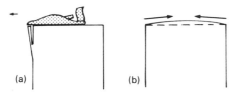

61   Planing end grain

The reverse edge

The width of the work is marked from the face edge at each end of the face side and reverse side and a longitudinal line cut on each side through the marks. Each end of the line on the reverse side should exactly coincide with the lines cut at right angles across the end grain from the longitudinal line on the face side. If there is more than about 10 mm ($\frac{3}{8}$ in) of surplus wood it is usually quicker to remove it with a saw to within about 2 mm ($\frac{1}{16}$ in) of the mark than to plane it off. The method of truing the reverse edge with a plane is similar to that used for the face edge. For precise work it is not sufficient to rely solely upon the marks. The edge should still be tested for squareness with the try square and for straightness with the straight edge.

Jointing
Planing true

If two pieces of wood are to be jointed edge to edge, each should first be trued on the face side and face edge, but not on the ends or the reverse side, and there should be a margin of thickness of about 3 mm to 5 mm ($\frac{1}{8}$ in to $\frac{3}{16}$ in) depending upon the overall size of the work.

It is not sufficient to true independently each of the edges to be joined. They have to be tested together to ensure that the two face edges exactly coincide longitudinally and that the face sides are parallel with each other.

The most convenient way of testing is to hold one piece of wood in the vice with the face edge uppermost and to balance the other piece on it, as

shown in figure 62. A light bulb or a torch shining from behind will show up any gap between the two edges while a straight edge held vertically against the face sides will show whether or not they are parallel with each other.

It is particularly important to check that there are no gaps at the ends of the boards, at (a) and (b) in figure 62, and also that the top board is firmly seated on the lower one. It is possible to have a tight join along the face side but a gap at one end of the reverse side so that one board can be rocked against the other. If the two edges do not fit satisfactorily it is generally better to make the necessary corrections to only one of them.

Some workers recommend that the two edges to be jointed should be squared simultaneously, so that if they are not perfectly square the two errors are cancelled out if the boards are reversed (figure 32).

The author has not found this technique effective for several reasons. In the first place, unless the wood is very thin, the plane blade may not be perfectly flat (figure 15) over the double width of the boards so that the edges tend to be slightly hollow. Secondly, the angle may not be consistent along the entire length in which case the two boards will rock when they are reversed, and finally, if there are any gaps between the two edges after they have been reversed, one edge will have to be planed separately, and it is difficult to maintain an angle which is not quite a right angle.

If the pieces of wood are edged on a shooting board these problems do not arise. One of the pieces, however, has to be trued on both sides so that it may present a true side against both the platform of the shooting board and the second piece of wood. This is necessary even if the two pieces are edged separately because, in order to compensate for any consistent error in the shooting board or the plane blade, one of the pieces has to be planed in the opposite direction to the other with, therefore, its reverse side on the platform of the shooting board.

Tonguing and grooving

Boards can be glued without tonguing and grooving but the amateur is advised always to tongue and groove for additional strength.

A groove is cut with a plough or combination plane about half way across the face edge and always from the face side. The groove should be about one third to one quarter the width of the edge and about 9 mm to 12 mm ($\frac{3}{8}$ in to $\frac{1}{2}$ in) deep. If the groove has to be cut against the grain the wood is liable to tear. This can be prevented by making two preliminary cuts with a cutting gauge along either edge of the groove.

The tongue is most conveniently made from a piece of plywood, preferably cut across the grain. The tongue should fit firmly but not tightly into the two grooves and has to be fractionally narrower than their combined depths. If the end grain will be visible in the finished work the last 75 mm (3 in) of the tongue should be made of the same wood as the work itself and cut longitudinally instead of transversely so that the end grain of the tongue matches the end grain of the board. The width of this end piece of tongue should exactly equal the combined depths of the grooves so that no gap is visible on the end grain.

After gluing, the new face side is re-trued and the other edges and faces planed to their final dimensions as described earlier in this chapter.

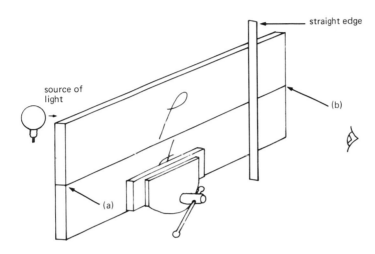

62   Testing an edge-to-edge joint

CHAPTER 6

Mortice-and-tenon joints

Types of joint

There are many versions of the mortice-and-tenon joint which is the one most commonly used in furniture making. Fortunately for the amateur it is rarely necessary to use more than a few variations of three main categories. In the first, or basic, category the mortice joint is cut parallel with the grain and some distance from the end of the wood. In the second category the mortice joint is also cut parallel with the grain but near the end of the wood, as in door stiles and table legs. In the third category the mortice is cut across the grain as in the tops of cabinets and the sides of bookcases.

Category I: Basic mortice-and-tenon joints

Three principal types of this category of joint are shown in figure 63. Type 'a' is a blind mortice which does not extend right through the wood. Type 'b' is a through mortice which extends through the wood and which is used when the tenon has to be held very strongly in the mortice as in a heavy door frame. Type 'c' is a double mortice which also gives extra strength, particularly against twisting, and which is used for bearer rails in cabinets.

Marking the tenon

The length of the tenon is marked on the wood (figure 64a), in the same way that the end of a board is marked for truing (page 53). The marks are cut fairly deeply with a sharp knife and must exactly coincide on all four faces if the shoulders of the tenon are to make a tight, flush joint with the mortice. The thickness of the tenon is determined by the width of the mortice chisel which should normally be about one-third the thickness of the wood. The pins of the mortice gauge are set to the exact width of the chisel, as in figure 64b, and the fence adjusted to the required distance from the face side. For most work the tenon and mortice components are of the same thickness and their face sides have to be flush with each other. The mortice gauge is, therefore, adjusted so that the marking pins cut approximately in the middle of the wood, as in figure 64c, and the same setting is used for marking both the tenon and the mortice, always from the face side. It does not matter if these marks do not exactly span the centre of the wood because the same degree of asymmetry will occur on the mortice as on the tenon.

If a through joint is to be cut and the tenon is

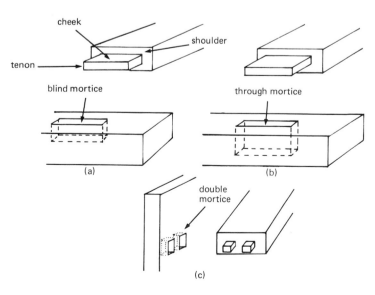

(a)   (b)   (c)

very wide it should be subdivided into two or more parts, as in figure 64d, to avoid weakening the other piece of wood with a long, unsupported mortice.

as in figure 65a, b and c. A small groove is then cut on the waste side of the shoulder mark with a chisel (as described below) to provide a guide, figure 65d, and the waste wood sawn from the shoulder.

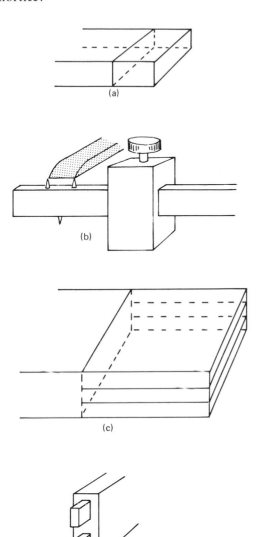

64   Marking a tenon

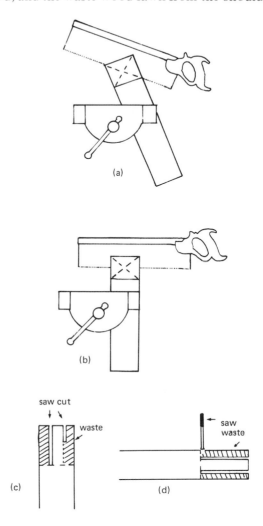

65   Sawing a tenon

Cutting the tenon

Professional cabinet makers cut tenon joints entirely with a tenon saw. The method is first to saw each side of the tenon from the end of the wood down to the shoulder and then to saw off the waste wood at the shoulder. This is done by sawing from each edge in turn, at an angle of about 45°, and then by sawing horizontally down to the mark,

The amateur, unless he is very experienced, may find it difficult to saw accurate tenons in this way. There is, however, a modified technique which takes longer but which always results in accurate work.

Instead of sawing exactly to the line, as in figure 65a, b and c, a very narrow margin is left outside the mark leaving the tenon slightly thicker than it should be. The waste wood is then cut from the shoulder not with a saw but with a wide chisel – the wider the better. The work is held against a stop at the left hand end, so that it will not slide on the bench top, and a small sloping cut made with the chisel against the shoulder mark on the face edge of the wood. Provided the mark was cut firmly with a sharp knife the small frill of wood can be brushed away with the fingers. The chisel is then held vertically with the flat side of the blade pressed firmly but carefully against the shoulder and lightly tapped with a mallet to cut the shoulder a little deeper. It is important not to hit the chisel hard at this stage because it might be forced back into the shoulder. A second sloping cut is then made with the chisel to produce a groove about 1.5 mm ($\frac{1}{16}$ in) deep. The same thing is done on the reverse edge and then on the face side but this time right down to the tenon (figure 66). As the groove becomes deeper the chisel can be struck harder without damaging the shoulder. The wood removed from the groove should be brushed clear so that it does not get underneath the work and score its surface. Finally, the waste wood is removed from the reverse side.

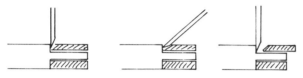

66   *Cutting waste wood from a tenon with a chisel*

Starting next on the face side the small surplus thickness of wood on the cheek of the tenon is trimmed off with a router plane, as in figure 67, the wood being held either in a bench hook or, better, with a bench holdfast. One half of the plane sole is held flush against the face side with the left hand while the right hand is used to swing the blade across the cheek of the tenon, care being taken to keep the movement of the blade perfectly horizontal.

A screw-adjusted router is the best tool for this job but a simple router can be used instead. To avoid splitting the edge, the far side of the tenon is cut down to the mark with a chisel before starting to plane, and the plane is adjusted to take a fine shaving. Although only a fine margin of wood remains, it may take several successive adjustments of the plane before it is all removed.

When the final adjustment has been made the plane is cutting the cheek of the tenon to its precise depth below the face side. This setting should therefore be used for all the tenons in the particular piece of work being made. There is a problem, however, because at the final setting the plane will cut too thick a shaving on the other tenons and will tear the wood. It is, therefore, really necessary to use two planes. If one of them is a hand-adjusted router it is better to set this to the final depth and to use the screw-adjusted router to remove all the wood except the final shaving on each tenon.

When all the face sides have been cut the process is repeated on the reverse sides. It is necessary to check that all the pieces of wood are of exactly the same thickness because if they are not the tenons themselves will vary in thickness if the same plane setting is used to make the final shaving on each one.

When all the tenons have been cut to the precise thickness they have to be cut to the correct width. This is marked on both cheeks of the tenon from the face edge with a marking gauge, as in figure 68a.

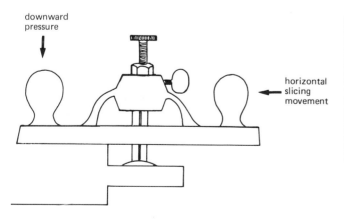

downward
pressure

horizontal
slicing
movement

(a)

(b)

67   *Trimming a tenon with a router plane*

68   *Marking and cutting a tenon to width*

The surplus wood is sawn almost to the shoulder with a tenon saw and cut away with a chisel by deepening the shallow groove already cut on each edge of the shoulder (figure 68b). With a double tenon the waste wood in the middle is also cut away with a chisel by working half way through the thickness from each face, care being taken not to tear the waste wood away from the end grain (page 65). The shoulders of the tenon have to be exactly at right angles to the sides and edges of the work. When the tenon has been cut it is cramped vertically in the vice and any surplus wood in the angle between the shoulder and the cheek is pared away with a bevel-edge chisel held horizontally with the bevel uppermost.

Marking the mortice
The sides of the mortice are marked with the mortice gauge but care has to be taken not to mark beyond the ends of the joint. It may, therefore, be necessary to re-mark the sides after the ends have been marked. If the face sides of the tenon and mortice are intended to coincide in the finished joint the sides of the mortice are marked with the gauge setting that was used for marking the tenon. If a different setting of the fence is required the marking pins are not moved.

Having marked, approximately, the length of the mortice the tenon component is aligned in its correct position with the shoulder of the tenon pressed firmly against the face of the mortice component and the tenon positioned at right angles across the mortice, as in figure 69a.

Two marks are then made at A and B with the point of a marking knife between the longitudinal gauge marks. The tenon is removed and with the try square butting against the face side, transverse

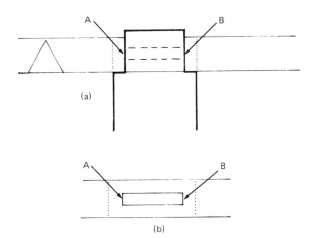

69 *Marking a mortice*

marks are cut with a firm pressure at A and B across the width of the mortice. The blade of the try square should be outside the transverse marks so that the thickness of the knife cut is inside the rectangle of the mortice. The longitudinal marks are then extended if necessary to the transverse marks (figure 69b).

If the mortice is to be cut through the wood the transverse marks are transferred to the reverse edge with a try square and sharp pencil and the mortice marked in the corresponding position on the reverse side with a try square and mortice gauge.

Cutting the mortice
A mortice is almost always cut into the edge of a piece of wood which may therefore need to be held upright on the bench. It is not satisfactory to cut a mortice with the wood held in a vice and if a number of joints are to be cut it may be worth making a rough jig to hold the work or, if practicable, to hold the work firmly in place with a cramp.

Some books describe a method of removing part of the waste wood with a brace and bit. This is not recommended. The amateur is likely to cut a more accurate joint with a mortice chisel alone.

The chisel is held vertically with the blade exactly parallel with the face side of the work, as in figure 70a. It requires some practice to prevent the blade leaning one way or the other as indicated by the dotted lines in figure 70a. It is advisable, if space permits, to stand in line with the wood and a try sqare can be stood on end to act as a guide.

Cutting should start in the middle of the mortice and the joint gradually deepened and extended towards each end (figure 70b). The mortice chisel tends to compress the wood as it cuts and the waste material has to be removed with a firmer or bevel-edge chisel which is a little narrower than the mortice. Special care is needed to avoid levering the chisel against the ends of the mortice and crushing the wood.

The mortice chisel can be struck quite hard with the mallet and it may be levered to and fro longitudinally to help remove the waste material, but it must not be allowed to twist and, again, care has to be taken not to damage the ends of the mortice. If there is any cross grain the successive chisel cuts should be very close together because the chisel tends to be deflected by the grain.

The wood is successively removed almost to the ends of the mortice. When this stage is reached the ends are cut with the chisel held vertically in both the transverse and longitudinal planes.

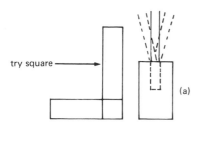
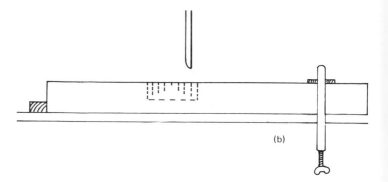

70　*Cutting a mortice*

The depth of the mortice is checked against the tenon with a combination square (figure 91). In the later stages of deepening the mortice a series of closely spaced transverse cuts is made with the mortice chisel and the waste wood scraped from the bottom of the joint with the narrower chisel. The ends of the joint can finally be trued by hand pressure with a sharp bevel-edge chisel the same width as the mortice chisel.

If the mortice is to be cut through the wood the joint is cut about half way through from one side and then finished from the reverse side. This ensures that the joint is parallel with the face side of the work. A through mortice can be opened out at each end of the reverse side to enable wedges to be driven in for additional strength, as in figure 71.

position. The joint is eased by paring very fine shavings with a wide chisel from the side of the mortice.

When the tenon is fitted fully into the mortice the joint is again tried for trueness by holding a straight edge against the face side of the mortice section and checking that the face side of the tenon section is parallel with it (figure 73).

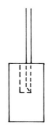

72　*Testing a mortice for trueness*

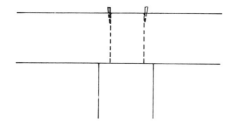

71　*Wedged mortice-and-tenon joint*

Fitting the joints

The tenon should not be forced into the mortice. If it does not go in with gentle pressure some easing is necessary, but before removing any wood it is a wise precaution to test the trueness of the mortice by holding a chisel blade firmly against each edge, as in figure 72.

If it is out of true the easing should, at the same time, correct the alignment but the top of the mortice on the face side should never be touched because this locates the tenon in the correct

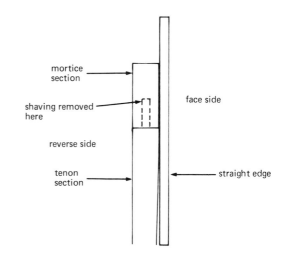

73　*Testing a mortice-and-tenon joint for trueness*

In figure 73 the tenon is not parallel with the mortice and a fine shaving has to be cut from the lower side of the mortice on the reverse side. The joint is not suitable for gluing until the mortice and tenon have been accurately trued. It is better for the joint to be slightly too loose than out of true, but if in the process of truing it becomes noticeably loose, one or both of the sections may have to be rejected. It is, however, sometimes possible to correct this fault (page 129).

Category 2: Mortice-and-tenon joints for frames and tables
Mortice-and-tenon joints for frames and table legs and rails are cut near the end of the wood and both the mortices and tenons differ in detail from the basic joint so that the tenon will not split the wood at the end of the mortice.
Marking and cutting the tenons
The tenon is positioned towards the inner (face) edge of the rail, as in figure 74a, to bring it away from the end of the door stile or leg. This leaves the outer part of the rail free to twist in relation to the stile. A shallow haunch is, therefore, left on the tenon which prevents twisting without unduly weakening the end of the mortice (figure 74b).

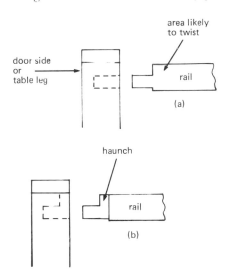

74   *A haunched tenon*

The positions of the tenon in relation to the thickness of the rail and the mortice in relation to the width of the leg can be varied, as in figure 75, according to the strength requirements and the design of the work. Within limits, the strength is increased by increasing the length of the tenon, as

in figure 75b and c, and the external appearance of the joint is influenced by the distance of the tenon from the face side of the rail. Very wide tenons are divided into two separate stubs (figure 64d) to avoid weakening the leg with two long and unsupported mortices joining at right angles. Tenons which fit into legs are mitred at the end, as in figure 75, to ensure the maximum area of contact between the tenon and the mortice.

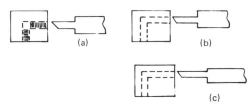

75   *Mortice-and-tenon joints in table legs and rails*

Marking and cutting the mortices
Some waste is left at the end of the mortice section to give added strength and is not removed until the joint has been glued. The mortice is marked in the usual way (page 59), except that an additional transverse mark is made at the end of the haunch. Unless the face of the tenon section is designed to finish flush with the face of the mortice section, the setting of the mortice-gauge fence is different for the mortices than for the tenons, although the setting of the marking pins remains unchanged.

While the mortice is being cut it is advisable to fix a small cramp across the end of the wood, as in figure 76, to prevent it from splitting. This is left in position until the joint has been cut and fitted.

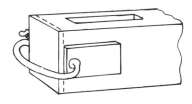

76   *Preventing a mortice from splitting*

When cutting mortices into two contiguous sides of a leg it is advisable to cut each side to the junction, as shown by the shaded area of figure 75a, before cutting either side to the full depth. This avoids the risk of tearing away the upper, inside edge of the first mortice when the second one is cut into it.

Category 3: Mortice-and tenon joints cut across the grain

The third category of mortice-and-tenon joint is used for the lateral jointing of wide pieces of wood such as the sides to the tops of cabinets, or bookshelves into the sides of bookcases (figure 77).

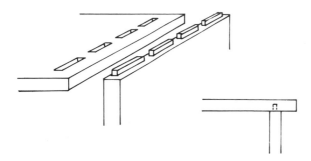

77 *Mortice-and-tenon joints cut across the grain*

Marking and cutting the tenons
The tenons are marked and cut in the usual way. Since the mortices are cut into the thickness of a board the tenons are relatively short and the width of each tenon is greater than the intervals between them.

Marking and cutting the mortices
The sides of the mortices are not marked with a gauge but with a marking knife against a try square or straight edge. The most reliable method on a wide board is to cramp one straight edge along the line of one side of the mortices and another parallel with it, along the other side. The precise distance between the two straight edges is the thickness of the tenon joints which can be used as distance pieces when cramping the second straight edge. If a try square is used the mark should always be cut with the blade of the try square outside the mortice.

The method of cutting the mortices is also different, a wide firmer or bevel-edge chisel being used instead of a mortice chisel. A frill of wood is carefully cut away from each side of the mortice, in the same way that tenon shoulders are cut (page 58), and the intervening waste wood removed at first with a chisel a little narrower than the mortice, and later with a router plane, as shown in figure 78.

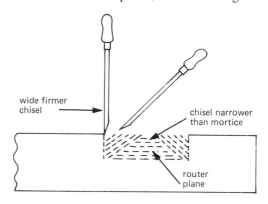

78 *Cutting mortices across the grain*

As the mortice is made deeper the chisel used for cutting down the sides of the mortice can be struck harder with the mallet without the risk of making the mortices wider. It should not, however, be struck very hard into a hard wood because, not being a mortice chisel, the edge is liable to chip.

As the mortice is progressively deepened the ends are cut down with the narrow chisel. The depth is checked against the length of the tenons in the usual way with a combination square (figure 91).

CHAPTER 7 Dovetail joints

Dovetails are the strongest joints for joining the ends of two pieces of wood at right angles face to face. There are three main categories: simple or through dovetails, lapped dovetails, and mitred or hidden dovetails. In the past, craftsmen believed that all joints should be hidden, and so the mitred dovetail was used to make flush joints of solid wood. Today, the lapped dovetail is accepted as an attractive feature of hand-made furniture, and there is rarely a need to use a mitred dovetail which, although not really difficult, is time-consuming to cut accurately. Simple or lapped dovetails, on the other hand, are easier to cut than one might at first imagine and pose no real problems for anyone prepared to take a little trouble. Simple dovetails are stronger than lapped dovetails and quicker to cut. They are used where strength is more important than appearance, as in the backs of drawers. Lapped dovetails are used where both strength and appearance are important as, for example, in drawer fronts and cabinets. Mitred dovetails, more as an example of craftsmanship than for necessity, can be used for flush-top cabinets, boxes and plinths.

Probably the most difficult part of cutting dovetail joints is the marking out, and the worker has, first, to decide:

a into which component to cut the dovetails and which the pins
b how many dovetails to cut
c how far apart to cut them
d what their angle is to be
e whether to cut the dovetails or the pins first
f for lapped dovetails, what is to be the length of the dovetails.

There are no unique answers to these questions and none of the decisions is absolutely critical. Whenever possible the joints are cut so that any pressure is exerted against the sides of the dovetails, as shown by the arrow in figure 79a. For this reason dovetails are always cut into the sides and not into the backs of drawers.

The greatest strength is achieved with a large number of narrow dovetails, giving a large glued surface area and with the spaces between the dovetails equal to their width, as in figure 79a where AB = CD.

There is obviously a practical limit to the number and, as a rough guide, fine work requires about one dovetail per 25 mm (1 in) of width and coarse work requires about one dovetail per 36 mm ($1\frac{1}{2}$ in) of width. It is usual to make the dovetails wider than the pins but, since the prime function of dovetail joints is to provide strength, the dovetail at its widest point should not be more than about twice the width of the pin at its widest point.

The angle of the dovetail is about 80° or 1 in 6. In softwood joinery the angle is usually about 5° more and in hardwood cabinet-making generally a few degrees less; that is to say the sides of the dovetails are more nearly parallel.

Some workers cut the pins first but the author has found it more satisfactory to cut the dovetails first and to mark the pins from them, except for mitred dovetails where the pins have to be cut first.

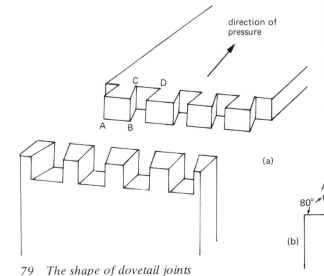

79 *The shape of dovetail joints*

Simple dovetail joints
Marking the dovetails

Marking dovetails is partly a question of trial and error and exact precision is not necessary, especially in simple dovetails which are rarely visible.

As an example there are five dovetails in figure 79b and the greatest width of each one is twice the narrowest width of the pins, therefore $AB = 2 \times BC$. The end pins are about the same width as the middle pins and BC is therefore $\tfrac{1}{16}$ of the total width. If the total width is 150 mm (6 in) the width of BC is 9 mm ($\tfrac{3}{8}$ in) and of AB is 18 mm ($\tfrac{3}{4}$ in). These distances can be marked off across the end of the wood with a ruler or a pair of dividers.

Alternatively, the approximate dovetail pattern can be drawn roughly to scale on a piece of paper and the widths of the end pins determined. These are then marked on each side of the wood, as in figure 80, and lines A and B drawn through the middle of the top of each one parallel with the edges of the wood.

A piece of wood or card, a little longer than the distance between the two lines, is marked with as many equal subdivisions as there are dovetails and placed diagonally across the wood so that the end marks coincide with the parallel lines. The position of each mark on the strip then coincides with the middle of each pin. These marks are transferred to the end of the wood with a try square and, with a little trial and error, the width of the dovetails is marked either side of them.

The length of the dovetails is equal to the thickness of the pins. It is sometimes recommended that the dovetails should be cut slightly longer to allow for trimming after gluing. This is not really necessary if the wood is planed square and true at the end and if the furniture components are cut to a full length. If the back of a drawer, for example, is cut to fit closely into the drawer opening it will have to be shaved off a little after it has been glued to ensure a smooth sliding action and this shaving is sufficient to clean up the joint.

The base of the dovetails, C–D in figure 80, is marked very lightly right round the wood either with a marking knife from the face edge or with a cutting gauge from the end (provided the end is perfectly true and square). The cutting-gauge cutter is set with the flat side away from the end of the wood, as in figure 81a, to give a sharp edge to the spaces between the dovetails. The cutting gauge is set against the thickness of the wood in which the pins will be cut but because the flat side of the cutter is facing away from the fence it is necessary to hold a flat surface against the far side of the wood (figure 81b), to ensure a correct setting.

When the base line of the dovetails has been marked round the wood the sides are marked, against a sliding bevel, with a sharp scribe or pointed blade from the end marks down to the base line, as shown in figure 82.

The sides need only be marked on the face side

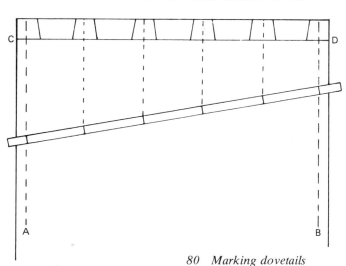

80   Marking dovetails

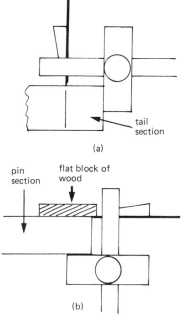

81   Marking the length of dovetails

of the wood and across the end, as in figure 82. After the dovetails have been marked the base line between them is cut more deeply with the cutting gauge as a preliminary to cutting out the waste wood with a chisel. It is a wise precaution to mark the waste wood with a pencil so that there is no risk of sawing the lines on the wrong side.

Cutting the dovetails

The wood is cramped vertically in the vice and each dovetail sawn down to the base line with a dovetail saw. The saw cut is made against the marking lines but with the width of the saw cut entirely in the waste wood. The worker has to concentrate simultaneously on keeping the saw blade at right angles to the wood and at the correct slope. The author has found from experience that this is most easily done if the saw is held with two hands and more attention paid to keeping the saw at right angles than at the correct slope. If the slope is wrong the dovetail will look less elegant but will nevertheless fit the pin which is marked from it, whereas if the angle is wrong the dovetail cannot fit properly between the pins. However, with a little practice, and by lining up the saw carefully before cutting, it is not difficult to cut dovetails at right angles and with the correct slope. When the cut is nearly down to the base line the saw has to be held perfectly horizontally to avoid cutting below the line on the reverse side.

When all the dovetails have been cut down to the base line the waste wood is removed with a chisel in much the same way that waste wood is removed from a tenon joint (page 58). If the base line was marked with a cutting gauge this can be used to make the preliminary vertical cuts into the waste wood in each side and each edge, as shown in figure 83.

A shallow groove is cut into the base line on the two edges to give a clean line in the finished joint and each section of waste cut half way through the thickness of the wood from one side and then half way from the other.

The waste wood is not entirely removed from one side because when the reverse cut is made it is liable to tear the unsupported waste away from the work. The cut is made instead in the shape of a V, as in figure 83. When the reverse cut has almost reached the base of the V, a sharp blow to the chisel will cut the remaining wood cleanly, with little or no tearing in the middle portion of the wood.

The end surfaces between the dovetails are finally trimmed with a chisel in the same way that the shoulders of tenons are trimmed (page 59). If one of the saw cuts has gone outside the mark into the waste it is possible at this stage to trim the dovetail down to the mark with a chisel, but care has to be taken to avoid making any curve in the side of the dovetail.

Marking the pins

The length of the pins is equal to the thickness of the dovetails and the base line for the pins is marked in exactly the same way as for the dovetails (figure 81).

The wood in which the pins are to be cut is held perfectly vertically in the vice with the face side

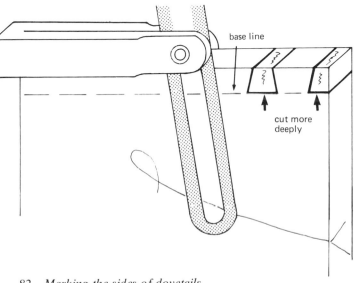

82 *Marking the sides of dovetails*

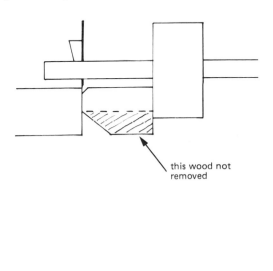

83 *Removing waste wood from dovetails*

outwards and projecting about 10 mm ($\frac{3}{8}$ in) above the top of the bench. The dovetails are then laid perfectly flat, face side uppermost, across the end of the wood, as in figure 84a, so that the length of the dovetails exactly spans the thickness of the pins. A small block of wood is put under the dovetail section to make it perfectly horizontal.

The two pieces of wood have to be aligned so that their face edges are in exactly the same plane and there are two ways of doing this.

If the top and front of the bench are true and square, a line AC (figure 84a) is drawn with a try square from the front of the bench and a coincident line AB with a try square from the top. The face edge of the pin section is aligned exactly along AB and that of the dovetail section exactly along AC.

The second method is to press the stock of a long-bladed try square along the top of the pin section so that the blade projects along the face edge of the dovetail section. The dovetail section is then moved until the face edges of the two sections exactly coincide at A, and the face edge of the dovetail section is exactly parallel with the blade of the square, as in figure 84b.

When the two pieces of wood are properly aligned the dovetail section is pressed down firmly in position with the left hand and the tops of the pins marked against the sides of the dovetails with the point of a knife or a sharp spike. It is advisable to go over the knife mark with a sharp, hard pencil to make it stand out more clearly, It is very

arm-aching to hold the wood firmly in position for long, and care must be taken not to move it if the pressure is temporarily relaxed. The strain may be eased by putting a heavy weight on the wood.

The pins have to be sawn very accurately to produce a closely fitting joint, but as soon as the first cut is made with the saw the mark is virtually obliterated. The author has, therefore, found it very helpful to repeat the marks, with a pencil only, about 2 mm ($\frac{1}{16}$ in) on either side of the original marks (figure 85). These act as effective guides when sawing. The guide marks can be made with a sliding bevel but the most accurate way is to re-position the dovetail section first to one side and then to the other of the original marks.

With the aid of a try square the pin marks are taken at right angles from the end down to the base line on the face side only, as in figure 85.

Cutting the pins

The wood is held vertically in the vice and the pins cut vertically down to the base line with a dovetail saw. As with the dovetails the saw cuts are made entirely in the waste wood, but contiguous with the marks, and they have to extend exactly to the base line but no further. Finally, the waste is cut away and the end grain trimmed in the same way as for the dovetails.

Fitting the joint

The pins are held vertically in the vice and the dovetails pressed into them with the two pieces of wood held at right angles to each other. It is

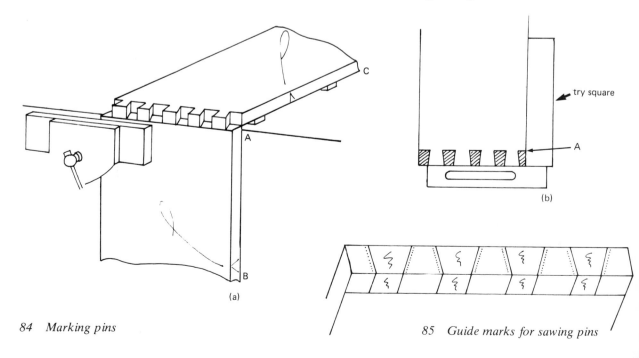

84 *Marking pins*

85 *Guide marks for sawing pins*

particularly important to check that the two outer dovetails are not exerting a sideways pressure on the two outer pins because it is easy to split the wood. Undue pressure can usually be detected by observation, or, after partially marrying the two halves of the joint, by looking for shiny areas on the sides of the dovetails or pins. Provided there is no pressure on the end pins it is safe to tap home the joint with light taps from a hammer or mallet onto a block of wood laid transversely across the dovetails (figure 86a). If the fit is very tight the joint is eased with a chisel where shiny marks appear on the sides of the pins or dovetails. When the joint is being tapped home all the dovetails should be kept at the same depth in the pins.

To dismantle the joint the dovetail section is laid flat on the bench, the vertical pin section lifted just off the bench and held firmly with the left hand, and a transverse block of wood placed in the right angle between them (figure 86b). The block is then tapped with a hammer, care being taken not to let the dovetails on one side come out faster than those on the other.

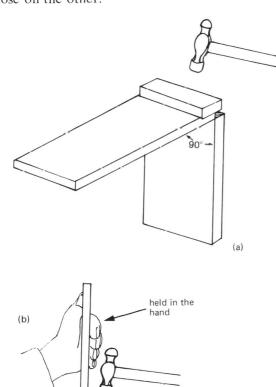

(a)

(b)   held in the hand

86   *Fitting dovetails into pins*

Marking
As soon as the two parts of the joint have been finally fitted they are marked as a matching pair.

Lapped dovetail joints
Figure 87 shows the use of lapped dovetails in the carcase and figure 88 in a drawer front of the military chest illustrated in figure 45. Although the appearance of the joints is important in these situations, strength is also a major consideration. The dovetails are therefore quite small, and in the carcase the dovetails and pins are of approximately equal width. The dovetails in the drawer are also only about one and a half times as wide as the pins. This is a deliberate departure from the convention of making the dovetails very wide and the pins extremely narrow in the fronts of drawers because the author prefers the strength and the workmanlike appearance of the more evenly spaced joint.

Marking and cutting lapped dovetails
The length of the dovetail in a lapped joint is the thickness of the wood less the thickness of the lap which is usually not less than about 5 mm ($\frac{3}{16}$ in). A cutting gauge is set to this distance with the flat side of the cutter outwards, as in figure 81b, and used for marking the base line (length) of the dovetails. Apart from this one point of difference the dovetails are marked and cut in exactly the same way as simple dovetails (page 64).

Marking lapped dovetail pins
The thickness of the pins is lightly marked on the end of the wood, from the reverse side, with the same setting on the cutting gauge as was used for marking the length of the dovetails. The length of the pins is equal to the thickness of the dovetails and no allowance need normally be made for trimming after gluing. The cutting gauge is, therefore, set to the thickness of the dovetails (figure 81) and the base line of the pins marked from the end of the wood on the reverse side only. The pins are marked in the same way as simple pins (page 65) except that the ends of the dovetails extend only to the back of the pins (figure 89).

Cutting lapped dovetail pins
The pins are cut with a dovetail saw as far as possible without cutting either into the lap or below the base line. The wood is then laid flat on the bench and the waste cut out with a chisel, almost to the lap, in much the same way that waste is cut out from one side of a simple dovetail pin (figure 83). The only difference is that the waste is entirely removed and not cut into a V.

87   *Lapped-dovetail joints in a carcase*

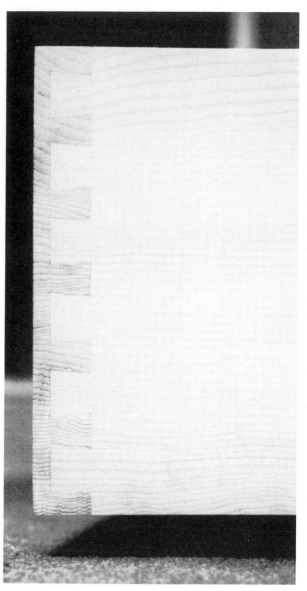

88   *Lapped-dovetail joints in a drawer front*

The wood is then fixed vertically in the vice with the dovetail slots facing the worker. The remaining waste is removed with bevel-edge chisels using hand pressure alone. A chisel narrower than the dovetail slot and with the bevel uppermost is worked horizontally to cut back the base while a chisel which is as wide as the depth of the slot is also worked horizontally, but with the blade on edge, to cut back the sides of the slot to the pin marks. The back of the slot is cut back to the lap with a series of fine slices cut vertically downwards with a chisel, as shown in figure 90. A very narrow chisel about 3 mm ($\frac{1}{8}$ in) wide is useful for clearing the bottom corners at the back of the slots.

When the slot is cut back to the pins on either side and to the lap at the back all three sides should be at right angles to the end of the wood (or parallel with its face). The trueness of the slot can be tested by holding the side of the chisel flat against each side and checking that it is at right angles to the end of the wood.

Checking the fit

The wood has to be cut sufficiently far back between the pins to accommodate the length of the

5 Yew record cabinet

6 Military chest of drawers made entirely of yew

7 African mahogany bow-fronted chest of drawers

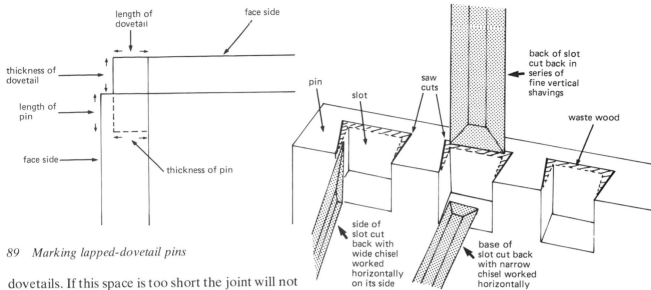

89 *Marking lapped-dovetail pins*

dovetails. If this space is too short the joint will not fit tightly together. The fit is easily checked by setting a combination square to the length of the dovetails, as in figure 91a, and then testing this distance between the pins, as in figure 91b.

Mitred dovetails
At first sight mitred dovetails look relatively complicated to cut, but the pins and dovetails themselves are really no more difficult than in an ordinary lapped joint. It is the mitre which requires special care if the joint is to fit accurately.

Marking mitres
Each piece of wood is planed true and square and to the same thickness and a cutting gauge, with the flat side of the blade outwards, set to the thickness of the wood (page 64). A mark is then made across the reverse side of each piece of wood, CD in figure 92a. Each end of this mark is joined to the end of the face side with a mitre try square thus forming the 45° mitre angle (figure 92).

There has to be a rebated lap in each piece of wood from which the mitre is cut. The precise size of the laps is immaterial provided they are identical in each piece. The rebates are marked as shown in figure 92 so that the distance of the rebate from the face side is equal to the depth of the lap, thus forming once again an angle of 45°. The cutting gauge is set with the flat edge of the cutter inwards for the mark on the end grain and outwards for the mark on the reverse side.

The normal way of cutting the rebate is with a tenon saw but the amateur worker is likely to make a neater and more accurate rebate if he cuts it with a chisel and router plane as if it were a tenon joint (page 58).

90 *Trimming lapped-dovetail pins*

The angle of the rebate with the reverse side of the wood can be tested for squareness with a combination square.

When each piece of wood has been rebated (figure 92b), lines are gauged parallel with the edges to allow for the mitres in the edges of each piece of wood. The width of these mitres is not

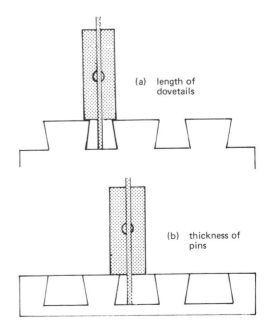

91 *Checking the depth of slots between lapped-dovetail pins*

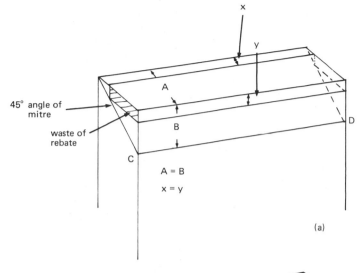

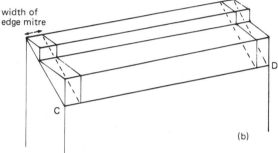

92   *Marking mitred-dovetail joints*

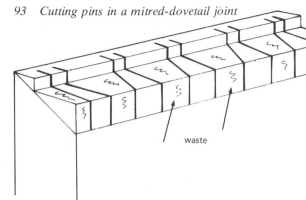

93   *Cutting pins in a mitred-dovetail joint*

easily cut with a chisel with the wood held on its side in the vice, as in figure 94.

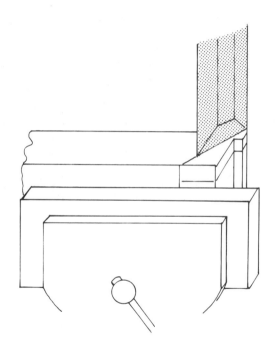

94   *Cutting the edge mitres*

critical but is something like 5 mm ($\frac{3}{16}$ in) for wood about 18 mm ($\frac{3}{4}$ in) thick. The same gauge setting is used for each piece of wood.

Marking the pins

The pins have to be marked and cut and the mitres cut before the dovetails can be marked. The ends of the pins are marked on the rebate, between the inner margins of the edge mitres, using a cardboard template cut to the shape of a pin. A sliding bevel cannot be used to mark the outline of the pins because it cannot be used in the rebate. The sides of the pins are marked with a try square down to the base line.

Cutting the pins

The saw cuts are made in the same way as for a lapped dovetail joint. It does not matter if the saw cuts extend into the mitre lap provided they do not reach the edge (figure 93). The pins are cut in the same way as for a lapped dovetail joint (page 67).

Cutting the pin mitres

The mitres are cut in the pin section after the pins have been cut. The mitres on the edges are most

Cutting the end mitre along the lap is probably the most difficult part of the whole operation and it is a great help to have a template cramped to the work with the end cut to exactly 45°, as in figure 95. Most of the mitre is cut with a wide, sharp chisel but it is finished with a rebate or shoulder plane, as in figure 95. The face of the mitre has to be perfectly flat and as well as being at 45° to the face of the work it has to be at right angles to the edge. These two angles are tested with a mitre try square and a try square in the course of planing.

95   Cutting the lap mitres

The mitre on the lap has also to coincide exactly at each end with the mitres on the edges.

Marking the dovetails
When the pins and the pin mitres have been cut the dovetail section is laid flat on the bench with the rebate upwards and the pin section held vertically above it in its correct relative position, as in figure 96. The outline of the dovetails is marked first with a sharp pencil and then, without moving the pins, with a sharp point to give a clear mark for sawing.

Cutting the dovetails and dovetail mitres
Both the sawing and the removal of the waste with chisels is done in the way described for lapped dovetails (page 67). When the dovetails have been cut the mitres are cut in the way described above for the pin mitres.

Checking the fit
If the joint does not fit tightly together the first thing is to make the check with a combination square described for lapped dovetails (page 69).

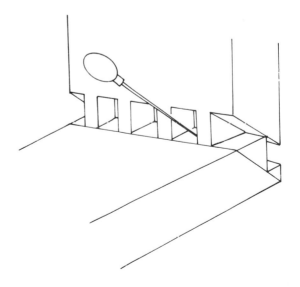

96   Marking the dovetails

97   *The strength of an unglued,*
mitred-dovetail joint

But in a mitred dovetail the pins as well as the dovetails have to fit into slots with a restricted depth. It is also necessary, therefore, to check the length of the pins against the depth of the slots between the dovetails. If the joint still does not fit tightly after doing these checks and making any necessary corrections, the fault must be in one or both of the mitres, which have to be tested with a mitre try square for the 45° angle, and with a try square, to see whether the face of the mitre is at 90° to the edge of the work. Figure 97 shows the strength of an unglued, mitred-dovetail joint.

CHAPTER 8

Constructing a work bench

It is not possible to do any serious work without a properly designed work bench, which needs to be strong, rigid and relatively heavy and to be equipped with one or two vices and an adjustable stop. It can be made of almost any species of timber but a softwood is almost always used because it is likely to be cheaper than a hardwood and is easily obtainable in the sizes required. Appearance is of little importance and secondhand timber of the right dimensions is suitable for the job.

The process of making a bench is good practice because it involves planing true, planing to thickness, and cutting mortice-and-tenon joints. It poses an obvious chicken-and-egg problem, however, because if one needs a bench there is presumably no bench on which to work. This is a very good reason for the beginner to join an evening class in order not only to build a bench but, more generally, to gain some initial experience in woodworking techniques.

The description below is based upon the author's own bench but there is no need to follow the precise dimensions. These are given as a guide only because the timber sizes depend in part on what is available while the dimensions of the bench depend upon the space available and one's height and personal preferences.

The legs and rails

The legs are made of about 70 mm by 70 mm (2¾ in by 2¾ in) timber, each end pair being joined by a 560 mm by 70 mm by 45 mm (22 in by 2¾ in by 1¾ in) rail at the top and another near the bottom, as in figure 98. The two rails are jointed and glued to the legs with through mortice-and-tenon joints, the top ones being haunched. The bench is about 760 mm (30 in) in height, so allowing for a 50 mm (2 in) thick top, the legs are about 710 mm (28 in) long.

The length of the bench is about 1780 mm (70 in) and the legs are set in about 150 mm (6 in) from each end. They are secured longitudinally by two rails at the back, one in the front, two top planks and one face plank. The longitudinal rails can be morticed into the legs, but if they are the bench cannot be dismantled, and since it is a large and heavy piece of furniture this may be a disadvantage. It is more usual, therefore, to fix the longitudinal rails with cross-halving joints which are screwed but not glued. Cross-halving joints are rarely used in cabinet making and are not, therefore, described elsewhere in this book but they are very easy to cut. A cross-halving joint is simply a slot cut across a piece of wood so that another piece can be fitted into it at right angles, as in figure 99. The width of the joint is marked with a

face plank 180 x 50mm
(7 x 2 in)

610mm (24 in)

180mm (7in)

50mm (2 in)

leg 70 x 70mm
(2¾ x 2¾ in)

760mm (30 in)

longitudinal rail
70 x 45mm (2¾ x 1¾in)

rail 70 x 45mm (2¾ x 1¾ in)

98   Cross section of a work bench

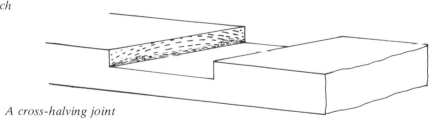

99   A cross-halving joint

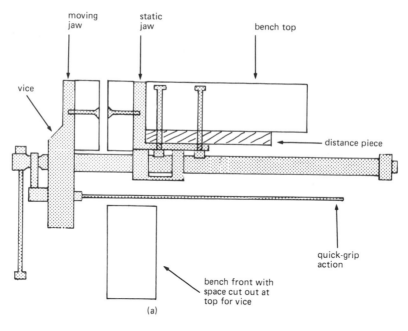

(a)

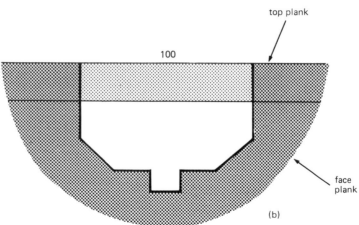

(b)

100   Fitting a bench vice

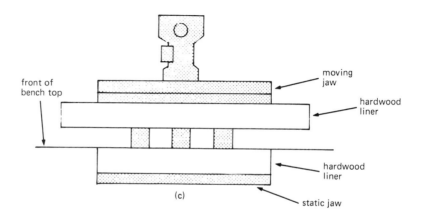

(c)

try square and marking knife and is equal to the width of the wood which is to fit into it. The depth, which is about 12 mm ($\frac{1}{2}$ in) is marked with a marking gauge and cut with a tenon saw. The waste wood is removed with a wide chisel by taking a series of thin shavings from each side, as indicated by the dotted lines in figure 99.

The longitudinal rails are also made of 70 mm by 45 mm ($2\frac{3}{4}$ in by $1\frac{3}{4}$ in) timber, and if they are fitted to the legs with cross-halving joints they should overlap the legs by about 100 mm (4 in) each end, making them about 1680 mm (66 in) long. Figure 98 shows how the longitudinal rails are screwed to the legs.

The bench top
The two top planks and the face plank, which are made of 180 mm by 50 mm (7 in by 2 in) timber, are screwed but not glued to the legs and top rails avoiding the mortice-and-tenon joints, as shown in figure 98. The top plank in the front is also screwed, at several points, into the top edge of the face plank.

The space between the top planks is filled with thin tongued-and-grooved boarding which is supported by the top leg rails near each end and by two or three transverse supports screwed onto the lower faces of the top planks.

The vices
Ideally, there should be two vices on the bench. For the right-handed worker the principal vice is positioned about 450 mm (18 in) from the left-hand end and the secondary vice about the same distance from the right-hand end of the bench.

There is some advantage in having a quick-grip action on the principal vice which allows the jaws to be opened or closed rapidly simply by releasing a trigger and without turning the handle. The principal vice should have jaws 180 mm (7 in) wide or more but 150 mm (6 in) jaws are suitable for the secondary vice.

Each vice is screwed, or preferably bolted, to the underside of the front plank, and in order to bring the jaws of the vice exactly level with the top of the bench a piece of wood may have to be inserted, as a distance piece, between the vice and the underside of the bench top, as in figure 100a.

A hardwood liner, approximately 25 mm (1 in) thick, exactly the same width as the jaw and extending downwards almost to the sliding base, is screwed to the static jaw, and the vice is positioned so that the face of the liner is flush with the face plank and its top edge flush with the bench top. This entails cutting a rectangular strip out of the

front edge of the top plank to accommodate the jaw and liner. A contiguous part of the face plank has also to be cut away to make room for the sliding bars and, if there is one, the quick-grip action. This is shown in face view in figure 100b. A wider piece of hardwood is screwed to the moving jaw of the vice, as shown in figure 100c.

Bench stop
An adjustable bench stop, which slides up and down through a square hole in the bench top, is positioned against the outside of the left-hand leg, as shown in figure 101. The bench stop is made of hardwood and is about 250 mm by 40 mm by 40 mm (10 in by $1\frac{1}{2}$ in by $1\frac{1}{2}$ in). It has a channel cut through it which slides over a coach bolt fixed through the leg. The stop is held in any chosen position by tightening the wing nut on the bolt.

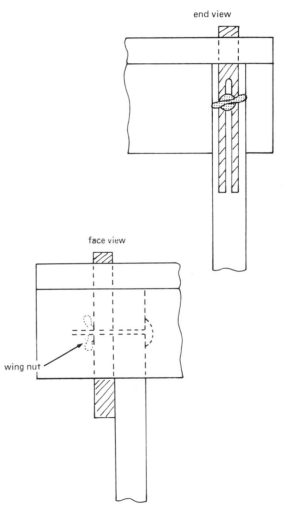

101   *Fitting a bench stop*

Bench holdfast
The bench holdfast is most conveniently fitted into the middle of the front plank of the bench. In order to give a better bearing surface it is advisable to screw a thickening piece of hardwood under the plank (page 35). A hole, into which the shank of the holdfast fits snugly, is cut at an angle of about 10° through the top of the bench, as shown in figure 28.

Diagonal supports
In order to give increased rigidity it is a good idea to screw diagonal supports between the back legs, as shown in figure 102. This leaves the front of the bench free for cupboards, drawers or shelving.

Screws and bolts
For the dimensions of timbers assumed in this chapter, the screws holding the planks to the legs and the top plank to the face plank need to be 75 mm (3 in) long and size 12. The screws for holding the longitudinal rails to the legs, through the cross-halving joints, need to be 60 mm (2¼ in) long and size 10. These dimensions allow about 25 mm (1 in) of thread to hold the wood.

All the screws and bolts are countersunk and liberally smeared with vaseline before insertion. The bolts which hold the vice through the bench top are countersunk below the surface of the wood to avoid any risk of damaging tools.

Lighting
Good lighting is as important as good tools, especially for someone who may wish to do much of his work in the evenings. It is particularly important to have the work well illuminated from behind but to one side of the worker. A good lighting combination is a powerful strip light on the ceiling over the bench, a movable lamp which can be clipped on to a shelf behind the bench and an adjustable spotlight behind and to one side of the worker.

Space
The amateur worker is lucky if he has adequate space in which to work. But however restricted the space may be, there must be room for a good-sized bench, and it is not really practicable to work in a part of the living area of the house. However careful and tidy one may be, woodwork inevitably makes a mess and creates dust, so the working area would have to be swept, dusted and vacuum-cleaned after each working session if one had to use a room which was also used for other purposes.

Health
Wood dust is rarely a serious hazard to health, but all dust is a minor irritant, and some species, such as teak which contains silica, can cause quite serious irritation to the nose and throat. Anyone, therefore, working for long periods with wood, especially if he is sanding in a confined space, is advised to wear a simple face mask which is obtainable at most chemists. After working, sanding dust should be cleaned up with a vacuum cleaner.

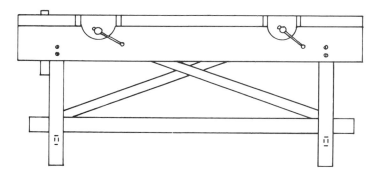

102   Diagonal bench supports

CHAPTER 9

Constructing tables

Three different types of table are chosen in this chapter to describe the basic methods of construction. These are a simple table, a table with a fitted drawer and a D table. They are illustrated in figures 39, 46 and 49.

A simple table

Much of the construction of a simple table is common to almost all types of table.

The top

The table top has, generally, to be made with several pieces of wood jointed edge to edge and then cut and planed true to size.

The underside of the table top is given its final finish with a scraper and abrasive paper before it is fitted onto the rails, but the top does not have its final finish until the table has been assembled. Any decorative edging, inlay or veneering has to be completed before the final assembly.

The rails and legs

The rails and legs are planed true and jointed with haunched mortice-and-tenon joints. If the legs are to be tapered the mortice joints are cut first, because a tapered leg is more difficult to hold firmly on the bench top while the joints are being cut. If the table is intended for hard wear and is more than about 1400 mm (54 in) long it is advisable to have a third transverse rail, as in figure 103, to stiffen the longitudinal rails and as an additional support to the top. This third rail is jointed to the longitudinal rails with stub mortice-and-tenon joints.

The top of the table is secured to the legs by wooden buttons which are screwed to the underside of the table top, but which are free to move in slots cut near the top edge of the rails (figure 104). This enables the large area of the table top to move, with changes in moisture content, without splitting.

The slots, which are about 25 mm (1 in) long, 10 mm ($\frac{3}{8}$ in) wide and 10 mm ($\frac{3}{8}$ in) deep, are cut before the rails are glued to the legs. They are marked with a mortice gauge about 12 mm ($\frac{1}{2}$ in) below the top of the rail on the inside and cut with a mortice chisel. The buttons are cut so that the height of the face is slightly less than the distance of the slot from the top of the rail. This ensures a tight fit when the button is screwed home, preferably with a round-headed screw. Each button is a little narrower than the slot and they are positioned

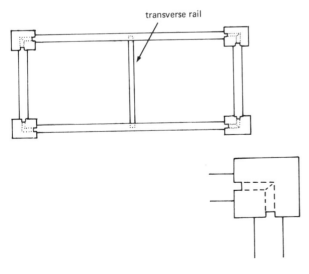

103 Top view of table legs and rails

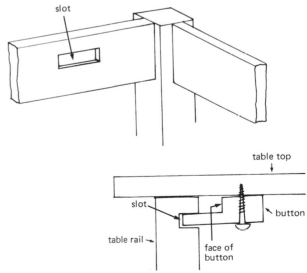

104 Button and slot

about 250 mm (10 in) apart. In an average sized table, therefore, there are about ten buttons, three on each side and two at each end.

Legs are usually tapered from the lower edge of the rail to the ends. The taper is marked on two opposite sides of the legs with a straight edge and marking knife, preferably with the straight edge cramped to the leg each time the marking knife is used. The corresponding lines are joined across the bottom of the leg with a try square and marking knife. The waste is removed with a panel saw and plane, the plane working with the grain from the top to the bottom of the legs. When the first pair of opposite sides has been tapered, the taper is marked on them for the other two sides and the waste removed in the same way as before (figure 105a).

The bottom of each leg is chamfered with a chisel to prevent the edge of the wood from splintering when the table is pushed sideways on a hard surface (figure 105b).

additional strength, and if they are slender it is made wider than the legs, as shown in figure 107, to provide space for the drawer stops. The drawer can be supported either on ordinary drawer runners, or on suspended runners (page 88), which prevent wear on the bearer rail and are probably, therefore, to be preferred.

If ordinary drawer runners are used they are morticed into the back of the bearer rail in the front and into the rail at the back. If suspended runners are used they are screwed and glued onto distance pieces which bring the inside of the side rails flush with the legs, as in figure 108a and b.

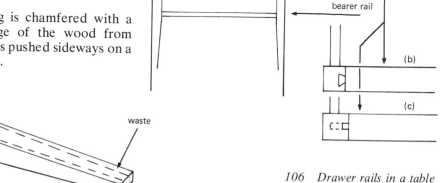

106   Drawer rails in a table

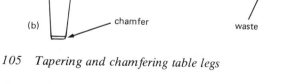

105   Tapering and chamfering table legs

Assembly
When the legs and rails have been glued, cleaned and scraped and sanded as described in Chapter 17, the top is fixed to the rails with the wooden buttons and given its final finish.

A table with a fitted drawer
The contruction of the top and of three sides of the rails is the same for a table with a fitted drawer as for a simple table but instead of the fourth rail there is a narrow top rail and a lower bearer rail, as in figure 106. Because it is so narrow and so close to the top of the legs, the top rail can either be dovetailed into the top of each leg or jointed with a haunched mortice-and-tenon, as in figure 106b and c.

The bearer rail is jointed to the legs with a twin mortice-and-tenon joint (page 56) to give

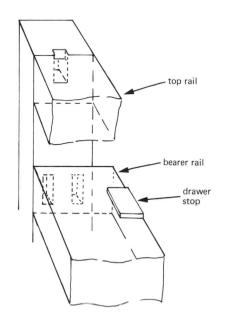

107   Bearer rails and drawer stops

Filling pieces are also needed, if ordinary runners are used, to act as guides to the sides of the drawer when it is being pushed in and out (figure 108b).

and the top, untapered portions scraped and sanded to bring them to their precise final dimensions. The positions of the legs are then

108 Runners for table drawers

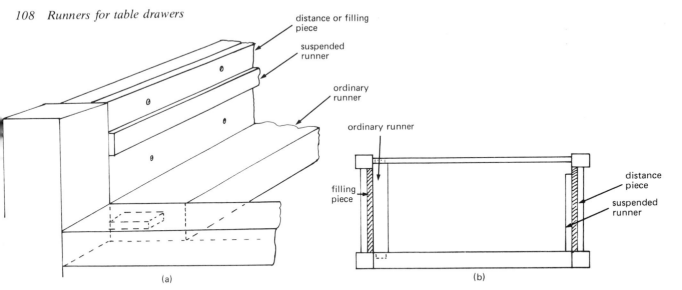

(a)   (b)

D table

The method of constructing the curved portion of a D table is the same as that used for making a round table.

The top

A rectangular top is prepared in the usual way and the curved shape drawn freehand with a soft pencil on the underside. When a pleasing shape has been drawn the next stage is to ensure that it is symmetrical. This is done by locating the mid point of the straight (back) edge and from it drawing radii at 10° intervals like a fan. The lengths of the corresponding radii, for example AB and AC in figure 109, are equalised and the curve re-drawn through the new points. Several successive adjustments are likely to be necessary before a smooth, symmetrical curve is achieved. The bulk of the waste wood is removed with a panel saw and the remainder with a plane. A block plane is the best tool for cutting across the grain at each end of the straight edge and this has to be worked away from the back edge to avoid splitting the wood.

The distance that the table top will extend beyond the rails is marked on the under side with an improvized gauge which marks with a pencil. A combination square and an ordinary pencil can be used for this purpose. The reason for this is to provide a pattern against which the curve of the rails can be tested.

The legs are planed to size, but not yet tapered,

marked accurately on the underside of the table top, as in figure 109. The spacing is a matter of personal judgment, but the space between the two front legs is generally wider than that between the back legs and the front legs, especially if a drawer is to be fitted into the front rail.

Marking and cutting curved rails

The straight back rail and the mortice-and-tenon joints with which it is jointed to the rear legs are all made in the usual way. The three curved rails in the front are cut from rectangular blocks which are first planed true and square (page 50).

When the block has been planed true and square the shape of the rail is marked on the top and bottom edges. This is most easily done by marking the outer curve of the table top onto a piece of stiff card which is then cut to the shape of the top. The slightly smaller curve of the rail is marked on the card in the same way that it was marked on the table top itself with the aid of a combination square and pencil. The card is then re-cut to the outer curve of the rail and is used as a template to mark the curve on the face edge of the block. The ends of the curve are transferred to the reverse edge with a try square and the curve drawn between the end marks on the reverse edge using the card again as a template. The thickness of the rail is then marked on each face using a pair of dividers or ruler to mark a number of points through which the inner curve is drawn. The ends of the inner curve are also marked on the ends of the block with a try square.

The inner curve is cut first. This is done by making a series of cuts about 15 mm ($\frac{5}{8}$ in) apart with a tenon saw from the reverse side almost to the line, as in figure 110. The waste wood is removed with a wide chisel and mallet by working, on the bench top, with the grain from each end towards the middle. When the waste has been removed almost to the lines the final cutting is done with a spokeshave. This requires very careful work and frequent testing with the try square to check that the back of the rail is flat and at right angles to the face edge. When the back of the rail is finished the bulk of the waste on the outer curve is removed with a saw and the final cutting to the line done with a plane, with the two edges of the rail held in the vice. The final shaping of the outside curve is tested against the curve drawn on the underside of the table top.

The rails are often veneered but the difference in curvature due to the thickness of the veneer is so small that it can be ignored. If the rails are to be veneered this is done before the joints are cut.

Marking and cutting the joints
Starting with the front rail and working on the underside of the table top the tenons are marked by aligning the top (face) edge of the rail along the curve marked on the table top so that the ends of the rail extend about two thirds of the way across the marks of the two legs into which it will be morticed. If the rail is too long at this stage it is cut roughly to length. The points at which the rail intersects the sides of the legs at each end are marked and joined across the face edge with a sliding bevel (the stock being held against the concave inner curve to prevent it from rocking). These marks are then continued across the width of each face with a try square and across the

reverse edge with a sliding bevel. If the rail is true the same setting of the bevel as was used for the face edge should exactly link the lines on each side across the reverse edge.

The problem now is to cut a straight tenon, at each end of a curved rail, which will fit into a mortice cut at right angles into the legs. A mortice gauge is set to the width of the mortice chisel and the two pins used to mark the base of the tenon on the face and reverse edges, as indicated by the points A, A¹, B and B¹ in figure 111a. The gauge is used from the outer (face) side and is lined up with the transverse marks. Lines are then marked across the leg marks on the table top corresponding in direction and distance apart with the mortice joints which will be cut into the legs themselves (figure 111b).

The outer of the two lines is the same distance from the curved line marked on the table top as the fence of the marking gauge is from the nearer of the two pins, distance (d) in figure 111b. In other words, points E and F in figure 111b are exactly contiguous with points A and B on the rail when it is in its correct position.

The rail is repositioned along the curve on the table top in its correct position in relation to the leg marks at each end (figure 111a) and cramped into position.

The points where the end of the rail intercepts the 'mortice' marks on the leg mark, points G and H in figure 111a, are marked on the rail and extended vertically with a try square to the reverse edge of the rail at points C and D. These are then joined to the original marks A¹ and B¹, which were made with the mortice gauge on both the face and reverse edges. This is repeated at the other end of the rail.

The tenons are now marked out and the cheeks

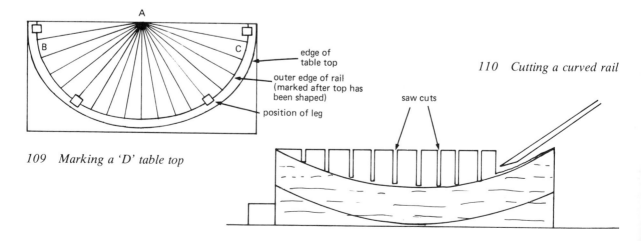

109   *Marking a 'D' table top*

edge of table top

outer edge of rail (marked after top has been shaped)

position of leg

saw cuts

110   *Cutting a curved rail*

111 Marking the tenon in a curved rail

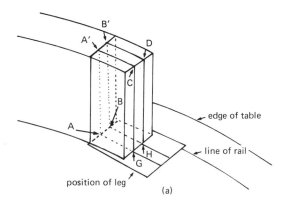

(a)

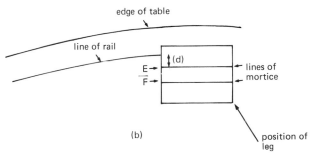

(b)

cut with a saw only. They cannot be finished with a router plane (page 58) because there is no level surface from which to use it. The shoulders, however, are cut with a chisel in the usual way.

Where two curved rails meet at a leg the mortice has to be cut straight through it. If the mortice were of the usual depth this would greatly weaken the leg. The tenon on the rail is, therefore, cut into two separate stubs and a corresponding double mortice

cut through the leg. From the point of view of strength it is better not to extend the top stub to the top of the leg with a haunch but to cut the mortice as shown in figure 112.

The opposing tenons are mitred at the ends so that they overlap each other in their common mortice.

When the tenons on the front rail have been cut at each end, the rail is cramped into the correct position and the positions of the leg marks checked before marking the side rails. This is done by butting the legs against the shoulders of the tenons, as in figure 113, and marking the side of the leg with a marking knife.

The side rails are marked, cut and jointed in the same way as the front rail, apart from the tenon into the back leg which is of the normal haunched type.

Fitting a drawer into a D table

If a drawer is to be fitted into a curved rail, an accurate rectangle has to be cut out of the rail after the tenons have been cut. The front and rear rails are cramped into position on the table top and a try square used to mark the position of each end of the drawer opening on the reverse (lower) edge of the front rail, as in figure 114. These marks are extended across the face side and reverse side of the rail with a try square and pencil. The top and bottom of the opening are marked from the face edge, which is resting on the table top, with a cutting gauge, the blade of which has to be reversed for the lower cut to ensure that the curved face of the blade is always in the waste wood (page 64). When the depth of the drawer opening has been marked in this way the pencil marks at each end are cut over with a marking knife.

The bulk of the waste is removed with a keyhole saw which is inserted through a hole bored near

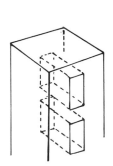

112 A mortice for two curved rails

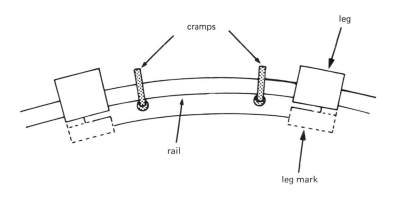

113 Checking the leg marks

one corner. The remainder is removed by very careful paring and slicing with a wide chisel, keeping one's eyes on the marking lines on each side of the rail. The trueness of the rail may be affected by the removal of the wood and needs to be tested after the drawer aperture has been cut.

The drawer runners extend from the front, curved rail to the rear rail. They could be jointed at each end with mortice-and-tenon joints but there are two reasons against this. First, there would be a great risk of splitting the wood if a mortice were to be cut across the grain at the end of the rail, outside the drawer opening. Secondly, because they have to be cramped with a Spanish windlass, the rails and legs of a D table cannot be glued as precisely as those of a rectangular table. If the mortices were

cut into the rear rail before gluing they could turn out to be perhaps 2 mm ($\frac{1}{16}$ in) out of true, It is, therefore, more satisfactory and easier after the legs and rails have been glued together to glue and screw runner bearers to blocks which are themselves glued and screwed to the front and rear rails, as in figure 115a which shows them in plan. The runners are then glued and screwed to the bearers, level with the top and bottom of the drawer opening (figure 115b). Alternatively, a suspended runner can be fixed along the middle of the bearer.

When the drawer and drawer stop have been fitted the drawer is pushed home and the drawer and rail sanded together (page 114) to obtain a perfectly flush fit.

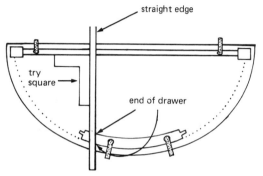

114   *Marking a drawer opening on a curved rail*

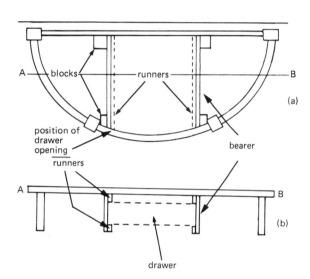

115   *Fitting drawer-runner bearers in a 'D' table*

CHAPTER 10

Constructing carcases

Types of carcase

A carcase is the framework for many types of furniture such as cabinets, chests of drawers, sideboards and bookshelves. It consists of a hollow box with a rebated back panel and an open front filled with doors, drawers or shelves, or a combination of all of them. It may stand on legs, on a plinth, or directly on the floor. There are two principal types of carcase. One is made of solid wood and jointed entirely with dovetail or dovetail and mortice-and-tenon joints. The other is constructed like a table with four corner pillars joined by rails at the top and bottom, which are jointed to the pillars with mortice-and-tenon joints. This type of carcase, in which not only the back but also the sides and the base consist of panels rebated or grooved into the pillars and rails, is generally more appropriate for fitted or painted furniture, and is dealt with in Chapter 18. This chapter is concerned only with the first type of carcase constructed of solid wood.

Flush-top carcase

A flush-top carcase, such as the framework of the military chest shown in figure 45, is jointed with lapped dovetails (page 67) on all four edges with the dovetails cut into the top edge of each side and into each end of the base and the pins, therefore, cut into each end of the top and the bottom edge of each side.

Overlapping-top carcase

If the top of the carcase overlaps the sides it is jointed to the sides with transverse mortice-and-tenon joints (page 62) but the base is dovetailed in the same way as a flush-top carcase.

Rebating for the back panel

A rebate is made wide enough to tack or screw a panel into the back of the carcase and as deep as the thickness of the panel which is to go into it. Many pieces of furniture are designed to stand against the wall in which case a hardwood-faced sheet of plywood makes a suitable backing. If, however, the back of the furniture is intended to be seen a framed panel, constructed like a thin door, can be fixed into the rebate with buttons (page 77).

The rebate cut into the top of the carcase is visible on the side if it is carried to the end of the

wood (figure 116a). The rebate, therefore, has to be stopped short of the end, as in figure 116b. This is done by cutting the end of the rebate, indicated by the shaded portion in figure 116b, with a chisel, thus allowing the rebate plane to cut to the point marked X without hitting the end of the wood at point Y.

The rebate can be carried through the entire length of the side of the carcase because neither end is visible externally and the gap at the bottom can be filled with a small piece of wood.

Shaping the front edges

If the front edges of the carcase are to be moulded or shaped with a plane this is done before the work is glued and, as with the rebating at the back, a chisel or gouge has to be used to shape the end which cannot be reached with a plane. Figure 118, for example, shows the end of the bevel at the top of a cabinet which has been cut with a chisel.

Fitting shelves

Shelves are generally morticed and tenoned into the sides of the carcase, or to vertical members within it, which are themselves morticed and

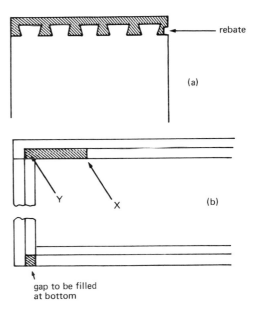

gap to be filled
at bottom

116 *Rebating a carcase for a back panel*

tenoned to the top and bottom of the carcase, as in figure 38. If the shelves need to be removed while the furniture is in service they can be supported on bearers, as in figure 117a, or, more elegantly, tongued at each end and fitted into grooved bearers which are screwed, or screwed and glued to the sides of the carcase (figure 117b).

117   Shelf supports

Fitting bearer rails and drawer runners

Bearer rails are morticed into the sides of the carcase with double mortice-and-tenon joints (figure 63c). If the edges of the carcase are bevelled, the bevelling is done before the mortice joints are marked out, so that the fronts of the bearer rails can be positioned exactly in line with the inner edge of the bevel (figure 118).

The tops of the drawer runners have to be exactly in line with the tops of the bearer rails. One way of ensuring this is to cut a short stub tenon on the outer end of each runner and to mortice it into the bearer rail. The runners can be aligned parallel with the top of the carcase and fixed with screws either before or after the carcase is glued together. If they have been tenoned, however, they cannot be glued until the carcase itself has been glued because the bearer rails cannot be inserted into their mortices with the runners fixed to the sides of the carcase. If the carcase is wide enough to use a hand drill and screwdriver it is easier to glue the carcase and bearer rails first and then to align the runners with their tenons in the bearer rail

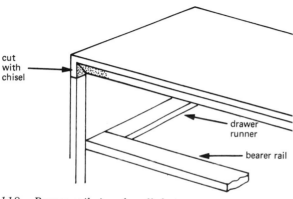

118   Bearer rails in a bevelled carcase

mortices, cramp then into position from the back of the carcase before the back panel is fixed, drill the screw holes and screw then into position. The screws and cramps are then removed to allow the inside of the runners to be glued before they are re-screwed into position.

It is possible to make a satisfactory job of aligning the runners against the bearer rail without a mortice-and-tenon joint and, therefore, to screw and glue them into position before the carcase is glued together. This is an advantage if the carcase is very narrow.

The carcase and bearer rails are assembled without glue and taking each bearer rail in turn a positioning block is cramped to it and the runner cramped to the positioning block, as in figure 119. The runner is aligned parallel with the top of the carcase so that AB = CD in figure 119, and the back of the runner is cramped to the side of the carcase. Holes are drilled and the runner screwed to the side of the carcase. The screws are then removed so that glue can be spread on the runner, which is then re-screwed into position.

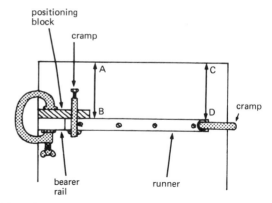

119   Aligning runners against bearer rails

Ideally, the drawer runners are screwed, with elongated screw holes, into grooves cut into the sides of the carcase. This exactly locates the runners, especially suspended runners, and allows the carcase to move independently of them. But, in practice, the author has not experienced any difficulty as a result of gluing the runners to the carcase although they tend to restrain tangential or radial shrinkage of the sides of the carcase (page 38). This is because the carcase is a relatively robust structure while the restraining effect of the runners is distributed over the whole length of each side panel. Gluing would be inadvisable, however, for furniture likely to be subjected to very wide fluctuations in humidity.

CHAPTER 11

Constructing doors

Frames

Construction

The frame of a hand-made cabinet door is made of two vertical stiles and two horizontal rails jointed together with mortice-and-tenon joints. These are usually haunched, as shown in figure 120a, but simple tenons can be used for light doors, as in figure 120b.

A door is not held in shape by other parts of the cabinet and is, therefore, particularly liable to move if there is any change in its moisture content. For this reason the stiles and rails should only be cut from straight-grained wood free from defects.

When they are being marked for cutting and jointing, each pair of stiles and rails is cramped together to ensure that they are perfectly matched.

The lengths of the stiles and rails are measured directly from the cabinet and a small allowance of about 2 mm ($\frac{1}{16}$ in) is added so that the door can subsequently be made to fit accurately by planing off the surplus wood where required, care being taken to preserve the symmetry of the door by planing each stile and each rail equally.

The frame can either be grooved or rebated to take the panel (figure 120c).

Grooving the frame

The rails are grooved along their entire length but the grooves in the stiles have to be stopped (figure 116) to prevent them showing on the top of the door. If, however, the tenons are haunched, the

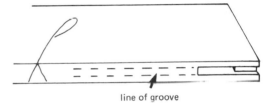

121 *Door-panel grooves*

stiles can also be grooved from end to end, because the groove is filled by the haunch of the tenon. It is convenient for the groove to coincide exactly in thickness and alignment with the mortice, but it can be thinner provided it runs through the space occupied by the haunch, as shown in figure 121.

Rebating the frame

If the frame is rebated instead of grooved, the rebate has either to be stopped short at each end of the stile, as in figure 122a, or the shoulder of the tenon has to be extended to cover the space which is shaded in figure 122a. Looked at from the top of the door, as in figure 122b, the cheek of the tenon on the face side of the rail is longer than that on the reverse side by the width of the rebate.

The amateur will probably find it more satisfactory to cut an end-to-end groove and to use a haunched mortice-and-tenon joint than to cut a stopped rebate or a rebate with an asymmetrical tenon.

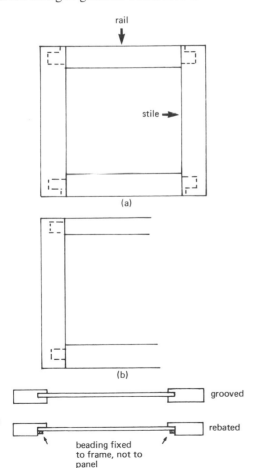

rail

stile ➤

(a)

(b)

grooved

(c)

rebated

beading fixed to frame, not to panel

120 *The construction of a door*

Grooves and rebates are always cut from the face side of the wood so that they are all perfectly coincident in the stiles and rails when the door is assembled.

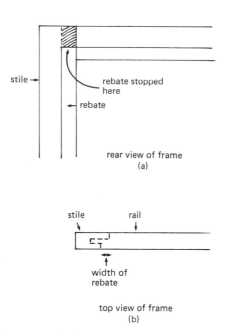

122   *Door-panel rebates*

Butt edges
If two doors close together they can simply butt edge to edge, as in figure 123a, or each stile can be rebated as in figure 123b. If they are rebated one stile has to be made wider than the other to give a balanced appearance to the front of the cabinet. Various forms of moulding can also be fitted, an example of which is shown in figure 123c.

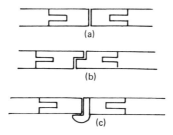

123   *Butt edges of doors*

Panels
Fixing
Panels are never glued or fixed rigidly to the frame but are free to move independently in the grooves or rebates (page 39). The beading which holds the

panel into the rebate is not, therefore, fixed to the panel but only to the frame (figure 120c).

The panel is made to fit firmly but not very tightly into the groove or rebate and to extend almost to the full depth. It can be expected to shrink a little from each side of the frame but not from the top or bottom.

Flush panels
Various types of panel can be made. A flush panel is illustrated in figure 40. This makes a tight joint at the top and bottom of the frame, but a longitudinal groove masks the shrinkage from each side. The panel is about 10 mm ($\frac{3}{8}$ in) thick and is set into a groove 5 mm ($\frac{3}{16}$ in) wide. The rails of the frame have to be cramped firmly against the shoulder of the rebate at the top and bottom of the panel while the door is being glued up. The raised portion of the panel has therefore to be perfectly rectangular and the rebate across the grain cut perfectly square without tearing the wood.

This is best done by making a deep mark with a marking knife against a steel straight edge, which is cramped into position, and then removing a deep frill of wood with a chisel, as described for a tenon joint (page 58). The waste wood is removed with a rebate plane set to cut a little inside the shoulder of the rebate, as shown in figure 124, to avoid the risk of tearing the wood on the shoulder. A chisel is used to clean up the waste not removed by the plane along the bottom of the shoulder.

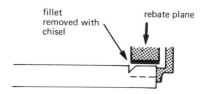

124   *Transverse rebate on a flush door-panel*

The longitudinal grooves, shown in figure 40, are marked with a marking knife to prevent any tendency for the edge to be torn away and then cut with a rebate plane along the edges and a plough plane in the middle. If a wide door is to be grooved in this manner the plough plane will not extend to the middle of the panel which has, therefore, to be made of two or more pieces of wood which are grooved before being glued together.

Bevelled panels
The bevelling is done with a plane after marking the inner and outer edges of the bevel on the face and edges of the panel. A marking gauge can be used for this, but the marks on the face have to be

very light otherwise they will show after the bevel has been cut. When cutting the bevel across the grain the plane has to be very sharp and finely set to avoid tearing the wood. The ridge formed by the bevels at each corner should be well defined and straight, and should exactly bisect the right angle.

A bevelled panel is often made with a central platform, as shown in figure 44. If it is cut from the solid wood the longitudinal edges of the platform are most easily cut with a plough plane and the transverse edges with a chisel. The bevel is then cut with a bench rebate plane which can cut closely into the lower edge of the platform (figure 125). A somewhat easier method is to cut the bevel first on a thinner piece of wood and to glue the platform onto the flat area between the bevels.

rebate the thickness of the 'groove' is determined by the position of the beading which is fixed in position after the panel has been bevelled.

Various forms of moulding can be fitted around the edge of the panel. An example of this is shown in figure 44 where a form of cock beading (page 96) is glued to the inner edges of the door frame.

All panels need to be cramped into position in the door frame before gluing to check that they fit properly.

Fitting
After checking for wind and then trimming, cleaning and sanding, as described in Chapter 17, each side of the door is fitted into its opening in the order shown in figure 127. After the initial fitting

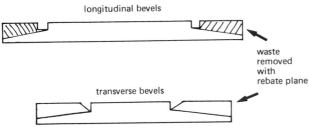

125   *Bevelling a door panel with a central platform*

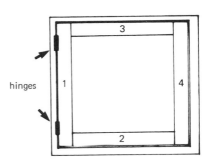

127   *Fitting a door*

A bevelled panel is easier to fit into a rebate than into a groove for the fairly obvious reason that the thickness of the bevel where it enters the groove has to be exactly the same as the width of the groove and this involves a certain amount of trial and error in fitting (figure 126), whereas with a

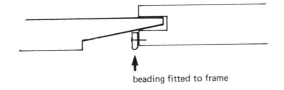

126   *Fitting a bevelled panel into a groove*

and before the hinges are put on there should be no gaps between the door and its opening. After the door has been hung on its hinges there is a final adjustment which usually involves some planing of the edges to ensure that there is a narrow gap of equal width on all sides. If the door is designed to fit flush with the front of the cabinet, the door and the cabinet are finally rubbed down together with abrasive paper after the locks or catches have been fitted (page 114).

Form of construction

The sides of a drawer are jointed to the front with lapped dovetails to mask the end grain and to the back with through dovetails. The bottom of the drawer is fitted into grooves ploughed into the sides and sometimes into the front and is tacked to the underneath of the back of the drawer.

The drawer usually slides on runners at the side and a bearer rail in front (page 84) and to reduce wear the bearing surfaces of the lower edges of the drawer sides are increased by gluing on hardwood fillets. If there are no bearer rails there is no space for ordinary runners and the drawer has to slide on suspended runners which fit into grooves cut into the drawer sides. The two types of construction are shown in section in figure 128a and b and also in figure 108.

The drawer should fit snugly into the drawer

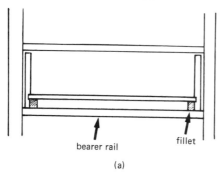

bearer rail   fillet

(a)

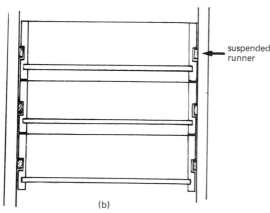

suspended runner

(b)

128 *Methods of supporting a drawer*

opening and there should be a gap of about 25 mm (1 in) between the back of the drawer and the back of the carcase to allow the air to escape when the drawer is pushed in.

The thickness of the drawer front depends partly upon the size of the drawer but is generally between 20 mm and 25 mm ($\frac{3}{4}$ in and 1 in). The sides and backs are generally about 10 mm ($\frac{3}{8}$ in) thick. The bottom of a drawer is most conveniently made from about 3 mm ($\frac{1}{8}$ in) plywood.

Marking, cutting and fitting the drawer front

The face side is always on the outside and the face edge at the bottom of the drawer. The drawer front is planed to fit accurately into the drawer opening before the dovetail pins are cut at the sides. It is cut slightly over-size with a saw and planed flat and to the correct thickness. The face edge and one side edge are then planed true and the depths of the left and right hand sides of the drawer opening marked on the respective sides of the drawer front. The marks are joined on the reverse side with a marking knife and, as an added guide, on the face side with a sharp pencil.

When the waste wood has been removed almost to these lines the drawer is tested in the opening to make sure that too much wood is not removed and that an accurate and very close fit is obtained. When the depth of the drawer front is correct it is partly inserted into the opening and the planed side edge is re-tested for trueness against the side of the carcase. If necessary, a few shavings are planed off to make it exactly parallel with the side of the carcase (figure 129).

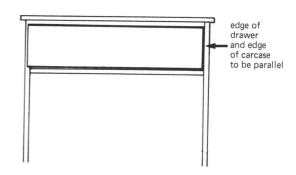

edge of drawer and edge of carcase to be parallel

129 *Fitting a drawer front*

When this edge is true it is inserted about 3 mm (⅛ in) into the opening and pushed hard against the side of the carcase, while the opposite edge is marked from inside the carcase and the mark taken right round the drawer front with a try square and marking knife. While the drawer is being marked in this way it is slightly askew because only one end is inside the opening and the mark is therefore slightly on the safe side. The waste wood is planed to the line with a block plane and the drawer tested in the opening. If it is a fraction too wide it is carefully eased by taking a few more shavings where required. When the planing is finished there should be a tight fit at each end and a firm fit at the top and bottom. The tightness is eased when the drawer is cleaned up after gluing.

If there are no bearer rails the drawer has to be supported on suspended runners. The depth of the drawer is not then marked from its opening in the carcase but is calculated and marked from the face edge with a marking gauge. Any cumulative error in depth is accommodated in the bottom drawer front which is best left unplaned until all the other drawers have been glued and fitted.

A bow-fronted drawer front is cut to shape from a rectangular block in exactly the same way as a curved table rail (page 80). The inside edges of the drawer front are left square, as in figure 130, to accommodate the sides. Since the process of

130   Shape of bow-fronted drawer front

cutting a curve from a rectangular block may relieve internal stresses in the wood some final adjustment may be necessary to obtain an accurate fit. To minimize this risk a curved drawer front should be cut only from a straight-grained piece of wood.

Decoration and fittings
Veneering or cross-banding is done before the drawer front is fitted into its opening. Cock beading is put on after gluing, cleaning and fitting. Lock recesses (page 126) can be cut into the drawer fronts after gluing but are more conveniently cut before the drawer is assembled. Catch recesses are

cut into the undersides of the bearer rails after the carcase is completed and the drawers finally fitted (page 126).

Most types of drawer handle are fitted after the piece of furniture is completed but the recesses for recessed handles, such as those shown on the military chest in figure 45, are more easily cut before the drawer is assembled.
Drawer sides and back
The lapped dovetails at the front and the through dovetails at the back of the sides together with the pins at each end of the back are marked out and cut as described in Chapter 7. Since the bottom of the drawer slides in its grooves under the back, the lower edge of the back is level with the top of the grooves which are usually about 3 mm (⅛ in) wide, 3 mm (⅛ in) deep and cut with a plough plane about 10 mm (⅜ in) from the lower edges of the sides.

The back of the drawer is, therefore, about 13 mm (½ in) shallower then the sides, and the dovetails at the back of the sides are marked out above the top of the groove, as in figure 131.

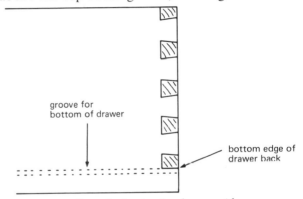

groove for
bottom of drawer

bottom edge of
drawer back

131   Dovetails at the back of a drawer side

If the drawer is to slide on suspended runners, grooves are cut approximately in the middle and on the outside of each drawer side, so that they end at the front between two dovetails, as shown in figure 132. They are about 10 mm (⅜ in) wide and about 3 mm to 5 mm (⅛ to ⅜ in) deep.

The grooves are cut with a plough plane, but to avoid grooving the dovetails, as indicated by the shaded area in figure 132, the front ends are cut first with a chisel and router plane. Each groove at the back of the drawer should, ideally, run through the middle of a dovetail, but this is not necessary, and if part of a pin projects into the groove it can be cut away with a chisel after the drawer has been glued together.
The drawer bottom
The bottom of a drawer has to be quite rigid and

for a large drawer the plywood needs to be about 5 mm ($\frac{3}{16}$ in) thick. This can be bevelled on the underside so that it fits into a 3 mm ($\frac{1}{8}$ in) groove. To give added strength with a wide drawer the drawer front is grooved as well as the sides, or, alternatively, a fillet of wood is tacked and glued to the inside of the drawer front below the bottom of the drawer.

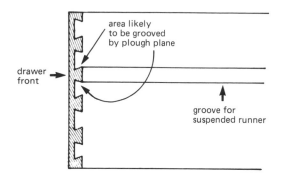

132   Grooves for suspended-drawer runners

The bottom is used to keep the drawer square while it is being glued together. It is cut very slightly too long, but perfectly square and to the exact width, so that when the drawer is assembled it will just slide in and out of its grooves. When the drawer has been glued, the bottom is tacked in position onto the lower edge of the back of the drawer, and the surplus length planed off to bring the bottom exactly flush with the back of the drawer.

Runner fillets
After the drawer has been glued together, squared hardwood fillets are glued to the inside of the drawer sides so that they are flush with the lower edges of the sides. These are to give a wide bearing surface on the runners and the bearer rail in order to reduce wear. The fillets also serve as an additional support to the bottom of the drawer (figure 128).

Fitting
Since the drawer is made to fit closely into its opening the final fitting after gluing involves very little planing and the normal cleaning up operation (page 112) is, in effect, a part of the fitting process. After the drawer has been glued together and the runner fillets glued to the sides, it is tested with a pair of winding boards to check that the lower edges of the two sides are exactly parallel with one another. If the drawer has been carefully made and glued there is unlikely to be more than a shaving or two to be removed from the bottom of one side and

the top of the other. The bottom shaving should, in theory, be taken from the rear portion of the side which is twisted downwards at the back. Sometimes, however, after gluing, the lower edge of one side may be slightly proud of the lower edge of the drawer front, as shown in an exaggerated form in figure 133, and the shaded portion has to be removed. This should be done before correcting for twist because it may reduce or remove the twist. Equally, of course, it may make it worse.

When any twist has been removed the sides are tested for trueness with a straight edge because they can become slightly distorted while they are being glued. Any inaccuracy can usually be corrected with a double-handed scraper (page 31) which is used to clean up the dovetails. The drawer is then pushed into its opening until the front is flush with the carcase. The crack between the drawer and the opening should be very narrow and of a constant width all round and some fine shavings may have to be removed from one or more of the edges to achieve this

Suspended drawers can be quite troublesome to fit. Each runner has to be parallel with the top of the carcase but no matter how carefully their positions are measured they are rarely in the exact position at the first attempt. It is, therefore, advisable to fit them temporarily in position with small panel pins which are easily removed. When each pair is correctly aligned a straight and square piece of wood is cramped against the lower edge of each one to act as a guide. The runners are then removed, glue is applied and they are then screwed or tacked back into position against the guides. If they have been moved slightly from an earlier alignment the position of the panel pins should be changed to avoid the risk of the pins locating themselves in the wrong holes in the side of the carcase. (See also page 84.)

Drawer stops
Small rectangular pieces of hardwood are screwed into each side of the bearer rail to act as drawer stops. They are positioned with the aid of a combination square which is used to measure the thickness of the drawer front from the front of the bearer rail, as in figure 134.

It is awkward to drill holes and to use a screwdriver in the confined space between two bearer rails but this method of fixing is recommended because, as with suspended runners, it is not always possible to locate the stops accurately at the first attempt. It is worth fixing them, deliberately, a fraction too far forward. The amount that needs to be removed, say, 1 mm

($\frac{1}{64}$ in), can then easily be judged after the drawer has been pushed right in. The stops are unscrewed and after the surplus wood has been planed off they are finally screwed and glued into position.

If a drawer has suspended runners, the runners themselves act as stops. They, also, should be fitted a trifle too far forward so that a small shaving can be sliced of with a chisel to obtain a perfectly flush fit.

Final sanding
The drawer front has to be flush with the carcase and the bearer rail. Any obvious projection is removed with a plane, but the final truing is done with a sandpaper block after the drawer stops have been fitted and with the drawer in the fully closed position (page 114).

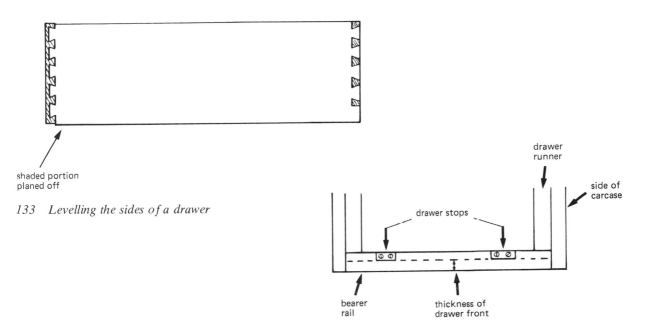

133 *Levelling the sides of a drawer*

134 *Drawer stops*

CHAPTER 13

Constructing plinths

A plinth is basically a hollow box with a rebate in the top to hold a chest or cabinet. It can either be plain, as in figure 48, or shaped as in figure 44.

Methods of jointing

Although dovetails are a perfectly acceptable structural feature in most pieces of hand-made furniture they do not look right in a plinth, and the problem is to hide the joints at each corner. There are three ways of doing this. The simplest is to mitre the corners and to strengthen them with internal glued and screwed blocks, as in figure 135.

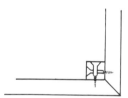

135   Mitred-plinth construction

The most craftsmanlike method is to use mitred dovetails which are strong and which appear from the outside to be simple mitre joints. But both of these methods have some disadvantages for the amateur. They entail the use of solid wood, which is expensive, and the simple mitre may open very slightly if the plinth shrinks more than the cabinet standing in it. The mitred dovetail is relatively difficult and time-consuming to cut accurately without considerable practice

A practical and effective method, which was used to make the plinths illustrated in figures 44 and 48, is to use lapped dovetails in front and simple dovetails at the back and to veneer the plinth with thin sheets of the same wood as was used for the cabinet. The front dovetails are lapped to avoid any risk of the shape of the dovetail showing through the veneer in the front of the plinth should there be any subsequent shrinkage of the wood in the plinth.

Shaping

If the plinth is to be shaped, this is done before gluing, and to achieve symmetry one half of the shape is cut from a piece of stiff cardboard and

used to mark first one half and then the other half of the complete curve. A coping saw is used to cut the waste almost to the line, and the final shaping is done with a spokeshave, chisel and rasp.

Rebating

If the plinth is made from solid wood, the rebate is cut before gluing. The plinth is cramped together without glue, the cabinet put into position on it, and the line of the rebate marked on the upper edges of the plinth. For most pieces of furniture the back of the plinth stands against the wall and the cabinet extends to the edge of the wood, which is not rebated, but is lower than the front and sides by the depth of the rebate (figure 136).

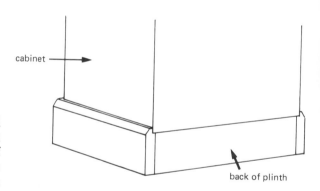

cabinet

back of plinth

136   Back view of rebated plinth

A difficulty arises if the cabinet is not perfectly square because it is not practicable to cut a rebate which is not parallel with the edge of the wood. The solution is to cut the rebate as wide as the narrower end, and to plane to the line at the wider end with a side-rebate or shoulder plane. With a mitred or mitred-dovetail joint the rebate does not have to be stopped but is carried to the end of the wood.

If the plinth is veneered, the rebate is not formed by cutting into the wood but by gluing a fillet of wood into position after the plinth has been glued and veneered (figure 137).

This method can also be used with a solid wood plinth because the glue line of the fillet is almost invisible, especially if the fillet is bevelled down to the glue line, as in figure 137. It has the advantage that a perfect fit is easily obtained even if the cabinet is slightly out of true. The fillets are mitred at the front corners of the plinth.

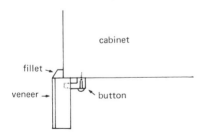

137 Rebate formed by a fillet

Veneering

It is assumed that the veneer, which is applied after the plinth has been glued and cleaned up, is cut to match the wood of the cabinet (page 94). It is, therefore, quite thick, about 2 mm ($\frac{1}{16}$ in), and has to be mitred at the edges. Each sheet of veneer is cramped in turn to its respective side of the plinth and marked with a marking knife on its reverse side against the edge of the plinth. This mark is extended at an angle of 45° across the top and bottom edges of the veneer and then down the face side. The waste wood at each end is sawn off just clear of the mark on the face side and the mitre cut between the marks on the reverse and face sides with a block plane.

This method has to be modified if the front of the plinth is curved, as in figure 48. The reverse side of the veneer is marked as described in the preceeding paragraph and if the curve is slight a 45° mitre is cut on the curved piece of veneer. This is then cramped back into position and the angle of the mitre on the side pieces of veneer judged by eye and marked on each side. The mitre will be slightly asymmetrical, but any discrepancy can be obscured by sanding a trifle more wood off the curved veneer in the final finishing stage. If the curve is pronounced, however, it is better not to cut a 45° mitre on the curved veneer, because the internal angle on the corner is not 90° but perhaps 120°, and if the front mitre is cut at 45° it will overlap the side mitre, as shown in figure 138a. In such a situation the angle of each mitre should be half of the internal angle, as shown in figure 138b.

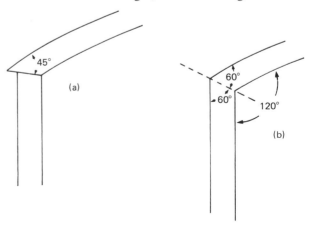

138 Cutting a mitre on a curve

If the plinth is shaped the mitred veneer is cramped in position and the shape of the curve marked on the reverse side with a pencil. It is safer not to cut the waste away until after the veneer has been glued to the plinth because it is very easy to splinter the wood. The object of marking with a pencil is to save gluing the area which will subsequently be removed. When the veneers have all been glued into position, the waste wood is very carefully removed with a coping saw, which should not be used very close to the edge of the curve. The remaining waste is taken off with a spokeshave, chisel and rasp.

If the carcase wood of the plinth is markedly different in colour from the veneer, it should be stained to approximately the same colour.

The rebate fillet is cut to size and glued into position after the veneer has been planed flush with the top of the plinth. If it is to be bevelled, this is most easily done after gluing.

Veneering

The use of veneer

A great deal of modern, factory-made furniture is constructed of board materials, such as particle board, covered with very thin sheets of veneer. This method of construction has been developed in response to rising raw material and wage costs, and much of it is well designed and well constructed, although it lacks the character of hand-made natural wood furniture. Veneers have often been used to cover poor workmanship, but veneering has also been a feature of high class cabinet making for over three hundred years, and the use of fine veneers to achieve decorative effects, which would otherwise be unobtainable, is a perfectly justifiable technique. It is also a somewhat specialized technique, the finer points of which are outside the scope of this book. There are, however, some occasions when the amateur may find it necessary or convenient to use veneers, either to achieve a particular effect or to complete a piece of furniture with a limited supply of scarce wood, and several examples of this are described in Chapter 4.

Preparing veneer

For the type of veneering described in this chapter it is almost always necessary for the veneer to match the solid wood of the furniture, and it has usually, therefore, to be cut by hand, although it can occasionally be produced as a by-product when a thick plank is being sliced by a local sawmill. Incidentally, a hand-cut or a sawn veneer shows the figure of the wood far better than many commercial veneers, which are sliced tangentially on a rotary cutter and often look rather featureless.

A piece of wood of approximately the required dimensions is trued on one side and given a completely flat surface with a scraper and abrasive paper. With care and patience a veneer of about 4 mm (⅛ in) thick can be cut with a sharp panel saw. The sawn surface is then planed with a sharp, finely set smoothing plane until the thickness of the sheet is reduced to about 2.5 mm (⅛ in). It is not possible to plane such a thin sheet against the bench stop because it is very liable to buckle and

crack. It is, instead, held by a bench holdfast and each half in turn planed from the middle towards the end of the wood.

Veneer of this thickness cannot be cut with a knife. The edges have to be planed true on a shooting board (page 35).

Cross banding

Cross banding consists of narrow strips of veneer cut across the grain and glued round the edges of a drawer front or table top (figure 46). There are two ways of cross banding. One is to glue both the centre panel and the cross banding to a prepared surface. The other is to cut a rebate round the edge of a prepared surface (page 86) and glue on only the cross banding itself.

To make the cross-banding strips, a wide piece of veneer is prepared and one edge planed straight and square on a shooting board. The width of the strip is lightly marked with a gauge and the strip cut off with a tenon saw about 1 mm (⅛ in) from the mark. This edge, which becomes the outside edge on the finished work, does not have to be made true because it will be planed square after the cross banding has been glued into position. Mitres are cut in a mitre block, but may subsequently have to be planed to ensure a perfect fit. This is most easily done on a mitre shooting board, but can be done on any shooting board with a piece of waste wood held firmly against the veneer to prevent the point of the mitre from splitting off. If there is a large amount of cross banding to be planed it may be worthwhile making a small-scale shooting board for use with a block plane.

Gluing

The methods of gluing hand-cut veneers are described in Chapter 16.

Moulded edges

Simple moulding

With a little ingenuity and fairly simple tools a number of different mouldings can be cut into the edges of tables and cabinet tops. The simplest to cut are chamfered and rounded mouldings, as shown in figure 139a and b.

The moulding is first cut along the grain because this forms a shoulder and prevents the end grain from splitting away when the wood is planed across the grain.

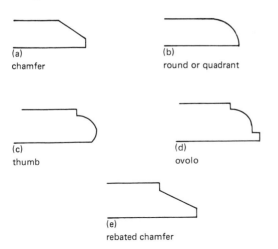

(a)
chamfer

(b)
round or quadrant

(c)
thumb

(d)
ovolo

(e)
rebated chamfer

139   Mouldings

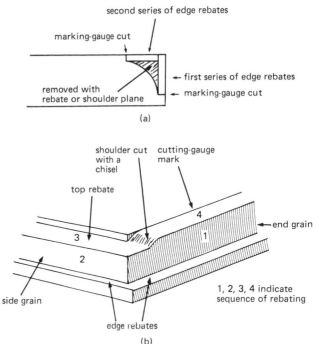

(a)

(b)

140   Cutting an ovolo moulding

Rebated mouldings

A series of somewhat more complex mouldings, such as the thumb moulding, ovolo moulding and rebated chamfer shown in figure 139c, d and e, are worked from an initial rebate or groove. Taking the ovolo moulding as an example, a rebate is cut along each edge and then around the face of the work, as in figure 140a. The sequence of rebating is shown in figure 140b. With the fence of the rebate plane set at the correct position, a nick is made with the blade in one edge, and the cutting gauge set to the width of the cut made by the plane blade.

A mark is then made as deeply as possible with the cutting gauge along each edge and round the face of the work in order to prevent the wood from tearing and to give a sharp edge to the rebate. When planing across the end grain, a piece of waste wood is cramped to the work to prevent the wood from splitting, and this is most easily done if the end grain is planed before the side grain.

When the edges have been rebated the face rebates are cut. If the fence now bears against the edge rebates and not against the original edges of the work, the reach of the plane has to be reduced by the depth of the rebate if it is to cut against the gauge marks on the face. When cutting the face rebates the order of cutting is reversed, and the planing is first done with the grain and then across the grain (figure 140b). This allows a shoulder to be cut with a chisel to prevent the wood from splitting when the rebate is cut across the grain.

The curve is cut with a rebate or bull-nose plane.

It does not matter which side is cut first provided the cross grain is cut from each end towards the middle. If the plane is set fine and the planing is carefully done the plane marks are easily removed, first with moderately coarse and then with successively finer abrasive paper. This can be held in the fingers and rubbed along the moulding, care being taken to avoid damaging the edge of the rebate. But a more satisfactory method is to cut a wooden template, with a gouge and rasp, to the shape of the curve, and to do the sanding with the abrasive paper held in the template (figure 141).

If a rebate plane is not available a plough plane can be used instead to cut a groove against the marking-gauge marks. The only difference is that there is more waste wood to be removed with the bull-nose plane after the grooves have been cut into the edges and face of the work.

Beaded mouldings

The beaded edge illustrated in figure 48 was cut with a beading cutter in a combination plane. The edges of the cutter were rounded with a file to give the profile shown in figure 142a and the moulding was finished with two small wooden templates and abrasive paper (figure 142b). With some species it is difficult to cut a clean moulding across the grain. To avoid the risk of tearing the grain in the

141 A wooden template for shaping ovolo mouldings

moulding, the table top illustrated in figure 46 was lipped with thin strips of yew, which were mitred at the corners. The mouldings were then cut into the longitudinal grain of the lipping on all four edges, as shown in figure 142a. The lipping is too thin to be easily seen in the finished work.

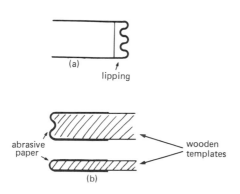

142 Cutting a beaded moulding

Cock beading

Cock beading is illustrated in figure 44 as a traditional moulding round the edge of a drawer. The beading is planed to a dimension of about 6 mm by 3 mm ($\frac{1}{4}$ in by $\frac{1}{8}$ in) and with the profile shown in figure 143.

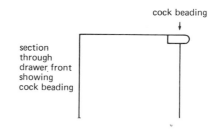

143 Cutting cock beading

The beading is glued into a small rebate cut into the edges of the drawer front after the drawer has been glued, cleaned and fitted into its opening.

The margins of the rebate are marked on the face and edges of the drawer front with a cutting gauge, and the rebates cut first along the top and bottom edges, with the fence of the plane bearing against the front of the drawer. Shoulders are cut with a chisel in much the same way as illustrated in figure 140b before the rebates are cut along the sides of the drawer. Before gluing the cock beading, which is mitred at each corner, the marks of the plane fence are removed from the front of the drawer with fine abrasive paper, because this is more difficult to do after the beading has been glued into position.

Inlaying

The type of inlay described in this chapter is of a relatively simple nature and is used for the restrained decoration of table tops and legs, as illustrated in figure 46 and 49.

Making the inlay

A piece of wood of a size suitable for the job is planed true and to a thickness equal to the width of the inlay. It is convenient if this is made equal to the width of the plough or router plane or chisel used to cut the grooves. A strip about 2 mm (⅟₁₆ in) thick is marked with a cutting gauge from the face edge and sawn off with about 1 mm (⅟₃₂ in) to spare. The sawn edge is then planed down to the gauge mark. A new face edge is trued on the original piece of wood and a second strip sawn off and planed true and so on until sufficient strips have been prepared. If shapes other than a straight strip are required, the wood from which they are cut is planed to a thickness of about 2 mm (⅟₁₆ in) and the shapes cut from it with the appropriate tools which are usually chisels and gouges. A method of marking a shape is described in the next paragraph.

Cutting the recess

After marking out the pattern of the inlay on the work with a pencil, a safe way of cutting accurate grooves for inlay strips is to cramp a steel straight edge along one side of the groove and to use the inlay itself as a distance piece for aligning a second straight edge along the other side of the groove (figure 144). With both straight edges cramped into position, the inlay strip is removed and marks cut deeply into the wood with a marking knife. The waste wood is removed to a depth a little less than the thickness of the inlay with the appropriate tool.

The best method is to remove the surface with a narrow chisel, leaving the straight edges in position, and then to cut to the required depth with a router plane if the plane blade is of the correct width. If a router plane cannot be used, it is possible to use a chisel alone, finishing off with a scraping action. A third method is to take away the straight edges and to remove the waste with the router/scraper illustrated in figure 23. If this method is to be used it is clear that the groove must be exactly parallel with the edge of the work or the edges of the groove will be torn by the scraper.

If curves or other shapes have to be cut it is possible to use the shaped inlay itself for marking the outline of the recess into which it is to be fitted. This method, however, tends to make the recess too large because the thickness of the mark is outside the inlay. It is preferable to make a hollow, or female, template which is used to mark both the inlay and the recess. The inlay is marked with a sharp pencil and the shape cut to the outside of the pencil line while the recess is marked with the point of a marking knife against the outline of the template, thus giving a good starting line for cutting the margin of the recess. For example, the reversed corners of the inlay illustrated in figure 46 were marked with a plastic template which was cramped onto the table top to mark each corner.

Fitting inlays

The inlaid strips are mitred at the corners and tapped into position (page 110).

Making a chess board

A chess board can easily be built up by gluing alternate pale and dark squares onto a flat surface, but if the board is to be decorative as well as

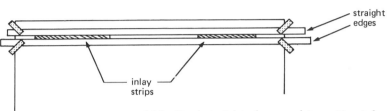

straight edges

inlay strips

144   Steel straight edges used in cutting inlay grooves

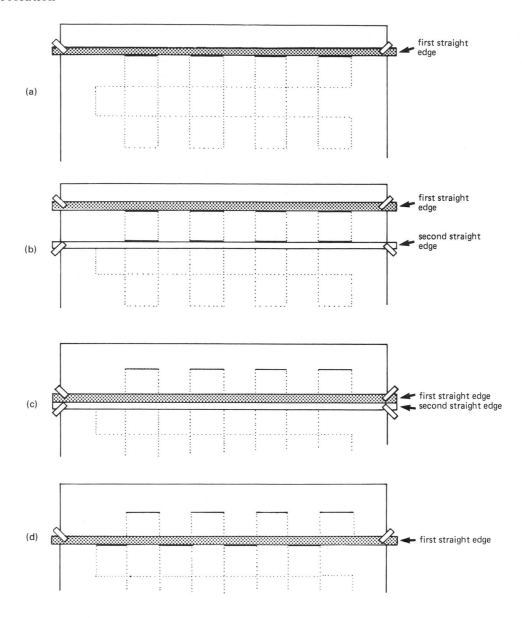

145 *Marking chess-board squares*

functional, as in figures 41 and 42, it is more effective to inlay the squares of one colour into a solid piece of wood of the other colour. This is a relatively exacting job.

Cutting the squares

A length of wood is planed true to a thickness of about 2 mm (⅛ in) and to a width equal to that of a chess square. There are two ways of cutting this into a series of squares. Since 32 squares have to be cut, it is worthwhile making a special jig for the job. This consists of a cross-cutting 'mitre' box

with a stop tacked or screwed into such a position that when the end of the wood is pressed against it the saw cuts a perfect square. This method does not work satisfactorily if the saw blade grooves have been widened by previous use. The blade must be precisely positioned by the grooves and have no room for lateral play. It is also preferable to use a shallow box so that a small dovetail saw can be used for cross cutting. The alternative method is to true one end of the length of wood and to mark off a square with a marking gauge.

This is then sawn off leaving a small amount of waste and trimmed to the line with either a wide chisel or a block plane on a small shooting board. This method, however, becomes very tedious after it has been repeated 32 times. Finally a small chamfer is cut along the four edges of each square on the reverse side so that it may easily be tapped into its recess without damaging the surface of the work.

Marking the board

The chess board is first marked carefully with a sharp pencil, starting from the centre of the board, and using a steel straight edge and a large square or protractor to draw the centre lines exactly at right angles. Two steel straight edges are needed for cutting the margins of the recesses with a marking knife because the lines cannot be cut straight along the rows. If they are, the squares do not meet exactly corner to corner, but overlap by the thickness of the marking lines. One straight edge is cramped into the position shown in figure 145a, and deep marks are cut along the margins of the first four recesses. When the four marks have been cut two of the squares, which have already been made, are used as distance pieces to align the second straight edge in the position shown in figure 145b.

After the four marks have been cut at the other side of the first row of recesses, as in figure 145b, the first straight edge is cramped against the second one, as in figure 145c and the second one removed. The second row of recesses is then marked as in figure 145d. This process is continued across the board and then repeated at right angles.

Cutting the recesses

The edges of the recesses are cut down with a wide chisel in the same way as the shoulders of tenon joints (page 58). The waste wood is carefully pared away, first with a chisel and mallet and finally with a small router plane. The depth of the recesses is slightly less than the thickness of the squares which are planed flush after gluing.

Fitting the squares

The squares are tapped into position (page 110).

CHAPTER 15 **Glues**

Properties required

Glue used by the amateur for furniture making has to satisfy several criteria. It needs to be strong enough for the job even in an imperfect joint. It therefore has to be a filler as well as an adhesive. It has to be relatively easy to use under home conditions and it is generally an advantage if it is colourless. It must retain its strength more or less indefinitely and so it has to be resistant to decaying organisms and, in temperate climates, to moderate changes in humidity and temperature. In some tropical regions a glue has to retain its strength over quite wide ranges of humidity and temperature and to accommodate considerable stress on the glue line resulting from movement of the timber. Generally, a furniture glue does not need to be resistant to prolonged weathering, to extremes of temperature or to the action of acids or alkalis. Within reason, expense is of only moderate importance because the glue used in a piece of furniture is likely to account for only a very small proportion of the cost.

The strength of glued joints

The principal strength of a glued joint is its resistance to shear, not to tension. The lap joint illustrated in figure 146 is very much stronger in the direction A than in the direction B.

The strength depends upon a number of factors which include the species and moisture content of the wood, the thickness of the glue line and the design of the joint. The shear strength of a well designed and well executed joint is greater than the shear strength of the wood itself.

In general, less dense woods glue more strongly than denser species, and oily woods, such as teak and iroko, are particularly difficult, especially if water-based glues are used. These difficult species are best glued immediately after the joints have been cut and the oil removed with a solvent such as methanol, although the oil can be removed later by washing the surfaces with a solvent before applying the glue. It is, however, a wise precaution with any species to sand lightly the surfaces to be glued if they have been exposed to the air for a considerable time or if, due to dull cutting tools, the gluing surfaces have become burnished.

All glues, no matter how moisture resistant they may be in service, are more effective if the wood is well seasoned at the time of application. The optimum moisture content for the types of glue likely to be used for furniture manufacture is about 12 per cent.

The thickness of the glue line is important. The thinner the glue line the stronger the bond and unless the glue contains a filler the glue line should not be thicker than 0.125 mm (0.005 in). Although a gap-filling glue can be used with a glue line not exceeding 1.25 mm (0.05 in) it is still preferable to keep the glue line as thin as possible.

All conventional wood joints are inherently well designed because they provide an adequate area of bonding, and they constrain the wood in such a way that it is virtually only a shear stress that can be applied to the joint.

Natural glues

Animal glues

Various types of animal glue derived from bone, skin and hide have been used from prehistoric times and no other types were available until about 1930. Many of these can make strong bonds but they are generally not resistant to decaying organisms, or to heat and moisture, and they tend to be troublesome to use. Animal-blood glues are moisture resistant if hot pressed and they are still used in some cheap plywood but almost the only animal glue still used today in furniture making is casein, which is made from milk curds. Casein glues are strong and easy to use and are moder-

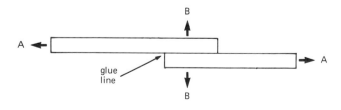

146 The strength of a glued lap-joint

ately resistant to heat and moisture, but they are likely to stain timbers having a high tannin content. They are no longer widely used because the synthetic resin glues are generally more satisfactory.

Vegetable glues
The only vegetable glue frequently used today is the contact-type glue which is made of rubber or synthetic rubber dissolved in a solvent. This type of glue is useful for bonding sheet materials together, but is not suitable for wood joints.

Synthetic resin glues
A number of synthetic resin glues have been developed since about 1930 and most of them are stronger and more resistant to heat and moisture than the natural glues. With the exception of the polyvinyl acetate glues, they all require a hardener to accelarate setting, although they will set very slowly without a hardener and therefore have a limited shelf life.

With some types of glue the hardener is applied to one face of the joint and the glue to the other so that setting does not start until the two faces of the joint are brought together. These are known as separate application glues. With combined application glues the glue and hardener are mixed in the correct proportions before use, while some glues have the hardener incorporated with the glue in the form of a powder. These are known as one-shot glues in which the hardener is not activated until the powder is mixed with water.

All of the synthetic resin glues, apart from the polyvinyl acetates, are thermosetting, which means that once they are set they will not soften again under the influence of heat. All synthetic resin glues set more quickly the higher the temperature but polyvinyl acetate, which is thermoplastic, requires a cooling period to harden before the cramps are removed.

The synthetic resin glues are all completely resistant to decaying organisms.

Phenol formaldehyde (PF)
Phenol formaldehyde glues are extremely strong and virtually indestructible. They will withstand more exposure, moisture and heat than the wood itself, and they form an extremely strong bond. The temperature has to be carefully controlled during the gluing process and for most types of PF glues a high temperature is required. They form a dark glue line.

Resorcinol formaldehyde (RF)
Resorcinol formaldehyde has similar properties to phenol formaldehyde but is easier to use and its only real disadvantages are its high price, which is

several times that of urea formaldehyde, and the fact that it forms a dark glue line. It is the only type of glue which is both completely water, weather and heat resistant and suitable for home use.

Urea formaldehyde (UF)
Urea formaldehyde is less strong and considerably less weather and heat resistant than phenol or resorcinol formaldehyde. It is, however, more than strong enough for furniture construction and is indefinitely resistant to the range of heat and moisture changes normally encountered in a building. It is colourless, and relatively cheap, and can be used at normal room temperatures, but should not be used below 10°C (50°F). A number of different types of urea formaldehyde glue are commercially available and they include separate application, combined application and one-shot varieties, some with a filler and some without.

Polyvinyl acetate (PVA)
Polyvinyl acetate glues are white, water-soluble emulsions. They can form bonds of high dry strength but are less strong than urea formaldehyde, and they are thermoplastic, which means that they soften in high temperatures. Although they re-set when the temperature is reduced, movement in the joint can rupture the glue line. They are not resistant to water but they are very clean and easy to use and have a long shelf and pot life. They form transparent glue lines. One of their disadvantages is a tendency to creep when subjected to sustained loading, but this is of little importance with most furniture.

Epoxy resin
Epoxy resins used as adhesives are combined application glues. The glue and hardener are stiff creams which are mixed together before use. They are strong and durable, and are used for bonding a wide variety of materials such as metal, wood, china and glass. They can be used for furniture making but are very expensive and have a short pot life once the two components are mixed together.

Choice of glue
Bearing in mind the qualities mentioned at the beginning of this chapter the most suitable types of glue for the home furniture maker are urea formaldehydes and polyvinyl acetates. Neither of them is particularly expensive, they both have adequate bonding strength under normal conditions and they both form colourless glue lines. They are also easy to use. Of the two types urea formaldehyde is probably the better and, being thermosetting, is unaffected by the

temperatures likely to be encountered in the home. Of the numerous forms of urea formaldehyde glue on the market the author prefers a one-shot gap-filling type, such as Cascamite.

For amateur work on large boats or for external structures there is no really satisfactory alternative to a resorcinol formaldehyde glue although a one-shot urea formaldehyde glue has been used successfully for a number of years on dinghies which are not continually immersed in the water and which are protected by paint or varnish.

CHAPTER 16 Gluing

Preparation

Need for assistance

It is essential to make careful preparations before gluing up a piece of furniture. Many hours of careful work can be ruined in minutes if the gluing is done carelessly or hastily. An assistant is essential for any but the simplest operation, and because the assistant is often likely to be one's wife, there should be a clear understanding that when the job is started it has to take precedence over all other household activities until it is finished. The operation should never be started until this has been clearly established.

Trial assembly

A piece of furniture containing many component parts should, if possible, be glued up in a series of steps, rather than in one operation. Few amateurs have sufficient cramps for a complex piece of work, and, moreover, the fewer the number of components glued at a time the easier it is to ensure that the work is true and square and that the surplus glue is completely removed before it hardens.

The first step is to assemble the work without glue and to check that the component pieces are numbered with a soft pencil which makes a clear mark without scratching the wood. There are two reasons for this preliminary assembling and marking. These are to check that one has had no mental aberrations, and cut a joint inside out or upside down, and also to prevent apparently identical components from being switched. Hand-cut joints, especially if made by an amateur, are not interchangeable. A tenon must fit into the mortice for which it was cut and trued and dovetails into their own pins.

Levelling the base cramps

Before dismantling the work it is convenient to use it as a guide in pre-setting the cramps to approximate lengths and in setting out the base cramps in their correct positions on the floor. Since few floors are perfectly flat the base cramps should be levelled to avoid twisting the work in the process of gluing. The levelling is done with a straight edge and a spirit level. The straight edge is put at right angles across the cramps, as in figure 147, first at one side of the work (a), and then at the other (b), and checked with the spirit level in each position. If there is any discrepancy between the levels the cramps are brought into alignment by raising one end of the uneven cramp or cramps with a piece of wood or card.

Equipment required

Before mixing the glue the rest of the gluing-up equipment has to be assembled. This comprises the following:

a   Wooden blocks to place between the work and the cramp faces. The blocks should be flat and smooth because if they are rough they will cause indentations in the wood. For some positions their length is unimportant but for others it is necessary to cut them to the correct length. This is illustrated in figure 148 where an upper cramp has to be positioned over the block.

In many situations, especially when one is short of cramps, the block has to distribute the pressure of the cramp over the whole length of

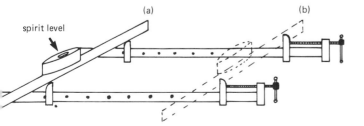

147   *Levelling the base cramps*

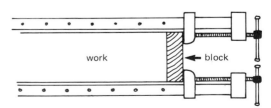

148   *A cramping block cut to length*

the work. This is shown in figure 149. In order to do this the block has to be reasonably thick and strong and it is sometimes worthwhile giving it a very slightly concave or convex shape. This is shown in an exaggerated form to the right of the figure.

b   Pieces of polythene sheet to prevent the blocks from sticking to the wood.

c   Wooden spatulas for applying the glue. These are easily cut to a convenient size and shape from a thin piece of wood. It is also useful to cut one or two extra spatulas for removing surplus glue from the inside corners of the work.

d   Damp cloths for removing surplus glue.

e   Sliding measuring sticks for checking that the work is square. These are used to test that the two diagonals of the work are the same length. The sticks usually have to be made for each job and consist of two flat, thin pieces of wood each of which is cut into the shape of a blade at one end. Each stick should be about three quarters of the length of the diagonals to be measured. They are held firmly in the hand, as shown in figure 150, and slid one against the other until they just fit across one diagonal of the work. The other diagonal is then tested and the cramp adjusted, as detailed below, until each diagonal is the same length.

f   A try square for checking that the work is square. This is occasionally useful, but for the reasons described below under the heading of cramping it may sometimes be misleading.

Gluing

Before mixing the glue, it is a sound precaution to have a trial run with the assistant to make sure that he or she knows exactly what to do. The glue should be applied fairly liberally to both faces of each joint and the work cramped gently together with a sheet of polythene between each block and the work. Any excess glue should immediately be removed with a wooden spatula and a damp cloth. Before gluing teak or iroko, the joints should be washed with methylated spirit to remove the oil from the wood and allowed a few minutes to dry.

Cramping

The precise positioning and alignment of the cramps depends upon the type of work and is discussed more fully below, but as a general rule all cramps should initially be aligned directly along the middle of the edges of the wood, as shown in figure 151a, although slight adjustment may subsequently be necessary to correct skewness, as described in the next paragraph. The cramps should also be parallel with the work in the other plane, as shown in figure 151b.

For most work it is unnecessary and undesirable to screw up the cramps very tightly because this tends to produce a permanent distortion in the finished article.

Squaring

The first thing to do after fixing and tightening all the cramps is to test with the measuring sticks that the work is square. Adjusting the cramps to eliminate skewness can be a fiddling and tedious process, but it is an essential operation, especially for a carcase that is subsequently to be fitted with drawers or doors. The method of adjustment is the same for any type of work and is illustrated in

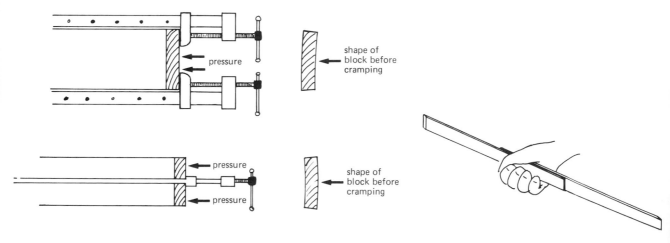

149   *Using a block to distribute cramp pressure*

150   *Diagonal measuring sticks*

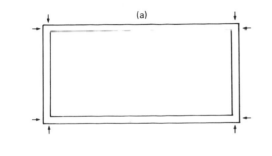

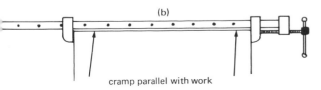

cramp parallel with work

151   Alignment of cramps

figure 152. In brief, the object is to turn a trapezium into a rectangle, and this involves applying diagonal pressure to the two corners of the longest diagonal, as shown in figure 152a. This is done by moving the cramps slightly out of alignment, as illustrated in Figure 152b. It is easy

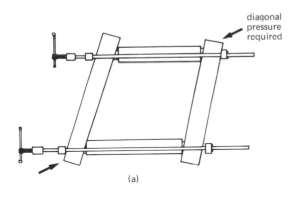

diagonal
pressure
required

(a)

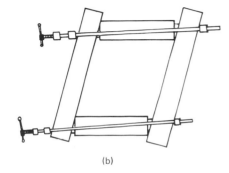

(b)

152   Squaring the work

to over-correct and a small adjustment is usually adequate to correct any skewness. There is usually a process of trial and error before the work is perfectly square.

A steel tape or try square can be used to test for skewness, but they are generally less satisfactory than the diagonal measuring sticks. It can be difficult to position and read a tape if there are several cramps in position and it is not really practicable to use a tape below the top surface of the work. This is of no importance for a door frame but is a serious disadvantage when testing a deep carcase. A try square has the disadvantage that it gives a misleading impression if there is any bending in the sides of the work due to the pressure of the cramps. This is illustrated in figure 153 where position 'a' suggests that the work is skewed in one direction and position 'b' that it is skewed in the other.

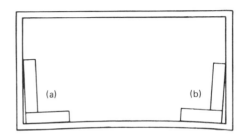

153   Distortion due to cramp pressure

Cleaning

The process of squaring the work may force some more glue from the joints. The final task, therefore, is to check that all surplus glue has been removed from the internal corners of the wood. Glue which hardens on the outside surface is an inconvenience but is easily removed. It is almost impossible, however, to remove hardened glue from inside corners without damaging the surface. The glue is best cleaned off with a fairly moist rag and a clean, chisel-shaped, wooden spatula which can reach right into the corners. The moist rag will raise the surface of the wood, but this can easily be smoothed off with fine sandpaper after the work has been uncramped.

Surplus glue

If the surplus glue is left inside its container beside the work it is easy to tell when it has set hard and when, therefore, the cramps may safely be removed.

Gluing particular types of work
Joining planks
If more than two pieces of wood have to be joined edge to edge it is preferable to glue only two pieces at a time.

The cramps are levelled on the floor, as described above, using one cramp for each foot or so of length. There should be one cramp within 75 mm (3 in) of each end of the work.

After applying the glue, the work is placed face side down on the cramps and it is advisable to kneel on the wood while the cramps are being tightened. This prevents any tendency for the wood to rise in the middle (figure 154).

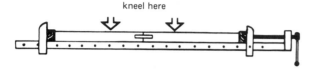

154   Cramping planks edge to edge

Door frames
Cabinet doors usually have rails only at the top and bottom and therefore only two cramps are required for gluing up. If the cramps are levelled and the joints trued before gluing, there should be no risk of winding – that is, distortion in the plane of the door. Although winding can be corrected by adjusting the cramps, as shown in figure 155, this is not likely to give a permanent correction, and it is really not advisable to glue up a door frame until any tendency to wind has been removed by adjusting the joints (page 60).

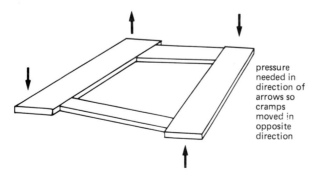

155   Correcting wind in a door frame

Before applying the glue the door should carefully be cramped together with the panel in position. This is done to check that the panel fits snugly but not too tightly into the grooves in the

frame and that the rails are aligned exactly with the end marks of the stiles because there is sometimes a small amount of possible longitudinal movement of the tenon in the mortice. The correct position is shown in figure 156a and the incorrect position in figure 156b. The frame has also to be checked for skewness (page 105) and corrected if necessary.

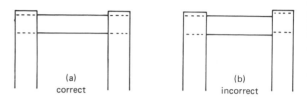

156   Alignment of the rail in a stile

Tables
Table legs and rails of square or rectangular tables are glued in three operations. Each pair of end legs and rails are glued separately and, when the glue has set, these are then glued simultaneously to the side rails (figure 157).

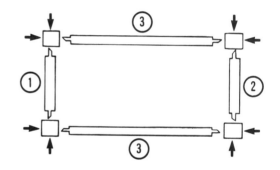

157   The sequence of gluing table legs and rails

Although only one cramp is needed for each pair of side legs it is advisable to level two cramps so that any tendency to wind may be detected and prevented. This is demonstrated in figure 158.

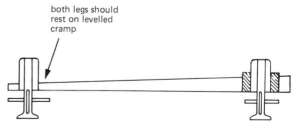

158   Preventing wind in table legs

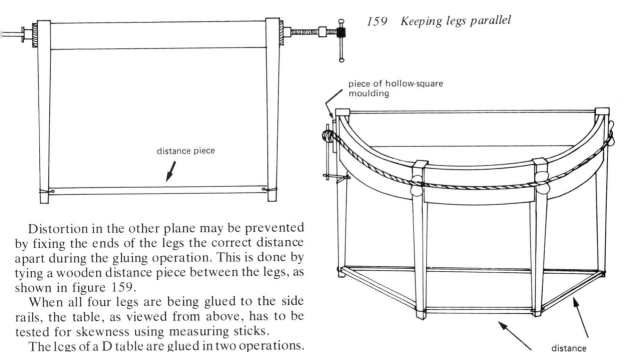

159 *Keeping legs parallel*

piece of hollow-square moulding

distance pieces

160 *Cramping the legs and rails of a 'D' table*

Distortion in the other plane may be prevented by fixing the ends of the legs the correct distance apart during the gluing operation. This is done by tying a wooden distance piece between the legs, as shown in figure 159.

When all four legs are being glued to the side rails, the table, as viewed from above, has to be tested for skewness using measuring sticks.

The legs of a D table are glued in two operations. The two rear legs and the straight rail are glued first in the usual way and the glue allowed to set. The three curved rails and the two front legs are then glued, assembled and fitted to the rear legs. The whole table is cramped with a Spanish windlass, which is a strong cord put round the top of the legs and twisted tight with a stick, as in figure 160.

A round table is cramped in a similar way with a Spanish windlass.

Carcases: general

There are three common types of carcase – cabinets, bookcases and drawers – and for each type the back or bottom, usually made of plywood, should be cut precisely to shape and placed, but not fitted permanently, in position before gluing up. This acts as a form of template and helps to keep the work square.

Most carcases are jointed with lapped dovetails and although it is possible to cramp dovetail joints in one direction only (figure 161a), it is preferable to cramp them in the other direction as well (figure 161b), especially if they form a feature of the work.

The joints have necessarily to be cramped together in the direction shown in figure 161a, but it is desirable to cramp also in the direction shown in figure 161b to achieve as close a fit as possible.

It would be useful to have ten or twelve cramps when gluing up the carcase of a large cabinet, and if bearer rails are also being fitted the number could

rise to fourteen or sixteen. This is far more than the average amateur possesses or can borrow, and economies have to be made partly by using strong blocks and putting the cramps further apart (page 104), and partly by cramping some components into position and then removing the cramps for use in another position. Although the direction of cramping shown in figure 161a is structurally more important than the direction shown in figure 161b, the joints are less likely to move from position 'a' than from position 'b' if the cramps are removed before the glue has started to harden. It is, therefore, possible to cramp dovetails sideways into the dovetail pins and then, if necessary, to remove one or more of the cramps for use elsewhere on the work.

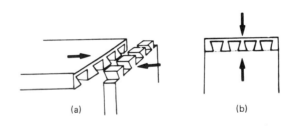

(a)   (b)

161 *Cramping lapped dovetails*

Carcases: cabinets

The base of a cabinet is almost always jointed with lapped dovetails but, depending upon design, the top may be jointed either with lapped dovetails or, if it overlaps the sides, with mortice-and-tenon joints. There may also be bearer rails fitted across the front of the cabinet with mortice-and-tenon joints.

If the top is morticed and tenoned, it is cramped in one direction only, but the bottom is cramped in two directions. The cabinet is positioned back down, longitudinally, on two levelled cramps (position 'a' in figure 162), with the back panel placed loosely in its rebate and the bars of the cramps exactly in line with the sides. Another pair of cramps (position 'b' in figure 162), is fitted in a corresponding position on the front of the carcase. If the carcase is deep and sufficient cramps are available, it is advisable also to cramp in position 'c' in figure 162 to ensure tight, flush joints between the sides and the top.

One or more cramps, if available, are fitted transversely at the base, as shown in position 'd' of figure 162.

If the top of the cabinet is jointed with lapped dovetails, the only difference is that transverse cramps are required at the top as well as at the base.

Ideally each bearer rail has a separate cramp, but it is possible, using strong blocks, to use one cramp for two rails. Thick blocks are in any case required to enable the transverse cramps to be positioned across the longitudinal cramps, as shown in figure 163.

Bookcases

From the point of view of cramping, a bookcase with movable shelves is a simple, shallow carcase. If it has internal morticed-and-tenoned shelves and partitions, it is necessary to cramp not only the outer carcase but also the internal shelves both at the back and at the front. This is shown in figure 164.

The lower shelf in figure 164 does not extend the full width of the bookcase but fits into a vertical partition. The back of such a shelf cannot be cramped until the back panel has been removed to make room for the cramp on the floor. This type of bookcase is cramped with the back panel in position, but after the work has been squared it is removed and a cramp slid sideways into position at the back of the short shelf (position 'a').

It is not practicable to cramp the back of the vertical partition because the transverse cramps on the floor are in the way. Instead, a sharp tap with a hammer where the cramp would have been exerting pressure were it possible to position it, will help to ensure a snug fit.

Drawers

A drawer is cramped in exactly the same way as a carcase which has dovetail joints top and bottom. The bottom of the drawer is slid into position before cramping, and particular care has to be taken to prevent it being stuck permanently by surplus glue.

The fillets, which give a wider bearing surface on the lower edges of the drawer sides, are glued into position after the drawer as a whole has been glued and uncramped.

Veneers: general

The description which follows applies to veneers cut by hand and includes inlays and chess boards. Because these veneers are hand cut they are likely to be at least 2.5 mm ($\frac{1}{8}$ in) thick, and, unlike the commercial veneers which can be cut with a knife and glued almost like paper, they have to be treated like thin sheets of wood and cramped into position, usually with G cramps. It is assumed that the amateur will use veneers only for cross banding or for surfacing plinths, bow-fronted drawers and curved table rails.

Veneers: cross banding

There are two ways of cross banding, as described on page 94.

If a central panel is to be glued to a prepared surface it can be troublesome to hold it precisely in position while the cramps are being applied. This difficulty may be overcome by marking the position of the central panel on the prepared surface and cramping two straight pieces of wood at right angles along two of the marked lines to act as guides for the panel (figure 165).

The panel can then be pressed against the guides while the cramps are being tightened. As soon as the panel is secure the guides may be removed and their cramps used on the panel itself. The most effective form of protecting block is a piece of fairly thick plywood cut approximately to the size of the panel. If it is markedly smaller than the panel the pressure of the cramp is not transmitted to the edges, while if it is larger it is difficult to remove the surplus glue. If the glue is not completely removed it is difficult subsequently to glue the cross banding.

The cross banding, which is fixed after the cramps have been removed from the central panel (or after the rebates have been cut), can also be troublesome to hold in position while the cramps are being applied. The answer to this problem is to press the cross banding firmly into position by hand and then to hold it in position with a strip of clear adhesive tape, having first removed the surplus glue. A strip of wood about the same width as the cross banding is put between the adhesive tape and the cramp faces to spread the pressure and to protect the surface of the work. It is advisable not to attempt to glue more than one strip of cross banding at a time. Any surplus glue at the end of each strip and especially at a mitre edge must be removed completely before it hardens.

Veneers: bow-fronted drawers

Because hand-cut veneer is relatively stiff it cannot easily be curved round a bow-fronted drawer or curved table rail without cracking. To prevent this from happening the inside of one drawer front can be used to hold a veneer in position against the second drawer front while it is being glued.

The slight difference in curvature between the front and back of the drawer is easily accommodated without permanent distortion, by the natural flexibility of the wood.

As many cramps as possible should be used to ensure a smooth surface on the face of the veneer. If too few cramps are used their positions can be detected after the veneer has been glued.

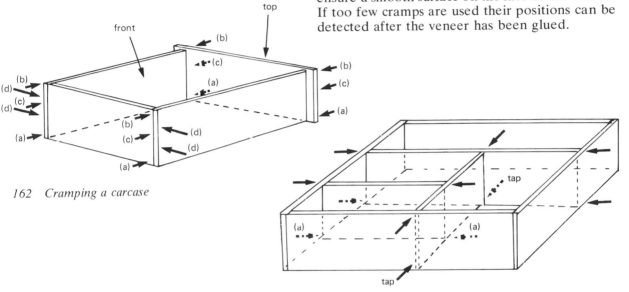

162   *Cramping a carcase*

164   *Cramping internal shelves*

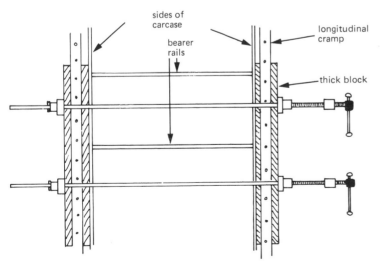

163   *Cramping bearer rails*

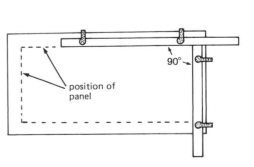

165   *Positioning a central panel*

Veneers: plinths
Each side of a plinth is glued separately and particular care has, therefore, to be taken to remove all surplus glue from the mitre edges. The best form of protection between the cramps and the veneer is a thick piece of plywood cut approximately to the shape of the veneer.

Veneers: inlay and chessboards
Inlay and chess squares should fit fairly tightly into their slots. It is usually sufficient, therefore, to tap them into position with a hammer or mallet using a firm flat piece of wood to spread the pressure and to protect the work.

Cock beading
Cock beading can be cramped into its rebate in two planes but it is sufficient to cramp in one plane and to use a weight in the other. This is illustrated in figure 166.

The block runs along the whole length of the work. As with cross banding, only one strip of cock beading should be glued at a time. Cock beading is sometimes used round the inside edges of door frames and can then only be cramped with square cramps (figure 167a). If the panel is bevelled it may be difficult to use cramps at all. But whether the panel is bevelled or not it is possible to hold the beading in position by a combination of weights and thin flexible sticks under compression, as shown in figure 167b and c.

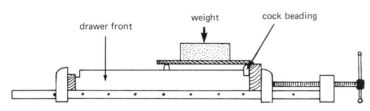

166   *Cramping cock beading to a drawer front*

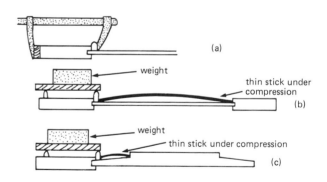

167   *Gluing cock beading in a door frame*

CHAPTER 17

Cleaning, sanding and finishing

Cleaning and trimming

Removing surplus glue

When a component or a finished piece of furniture is uncramped after gluing the surplus glue has to be cleaned off. All the glue should have been removed from the internal surfaces during the gluing up process but in practice there is usually some final cleaning to be done. When glue is wiped off with a damp rag, a fine film is often left behind, and this is easily sanded off with fine garnet or flour paper wrapped round a chisel-shaped sanding block (figure 168a). If a thicker deposit of glue has been overlooked or has oozed out of a crack it is more effectively removed with a scraper, as in figure 168b, or a sharp knife. If the edge of the knife is pressed into the angle of the joint, as in figure 168c, the glue can often be made to split away from the wood.

Glue on external surfaces, below the cramping blocks, is usually taken off with a plane, but the best tool for cleaning up dovetail joints is a double-handed scraper. A drawer, for example, is supported in such a way that it is not subjected to any diagonal stress, and the scraper, held diagonally to the direction of the grain, is worked inwards from the edge of the wood (figure 169).

Trimming joints

The waste pieces which are left at each end of door stiles or at the top of table legs are cut off close to the rails with a fine tenon saw and then planed flush with the rails. The inner edge of a table leg is cut to the line with a chisel to prevent splitting when it is planed (figure 170).

Large discrepancies between the sides or edges of adjoining components which should be flush with one another are the result of inaccurate joints, usually mortice-and-tenon joints. This type of discrepancy can only be regarded as a mistake and is discussed in Chapter 20. Very small discrepancies, however, of about 1 mm ($\frac{1}{32}$ in) or less between, for example, the stiles and rails of a door frame, or the top, sides and bearer rails of a cabinet, can be regarded as normal and have to be planed flush. Abrasive paper should not be used because it tends to blur the precision of the work (figure 171).

This operation of trimming the joints may put the whole work very slightly out of true, so that the frames of doors or the fronts of drawers will not be exactly flush with their openings. The whole work has, therefore, to be tested for trueness with a straight edge and spirit level, or with winding strips, and any distortion corrected with a smoothing plane. Special care is needed in doing this to avoid planing across the edges and splitting off slivers of wood.

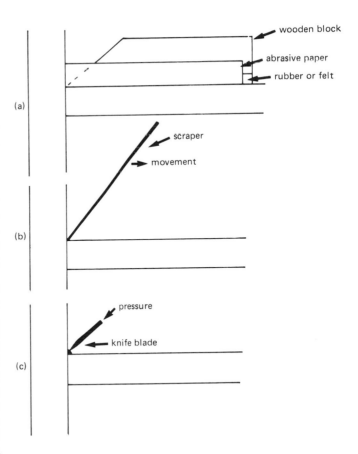

168   Removing dried glue

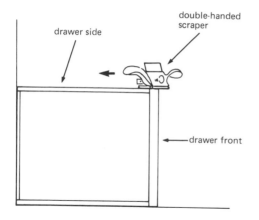

169   Cleaning dovetail joints in a drawer

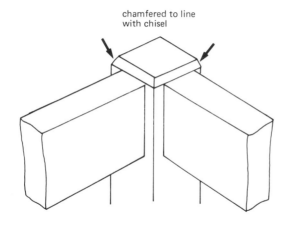

170   Planing waste from a table leg

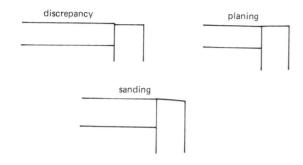

171   Trimming discrepancy in edges

Sanding

Sanding is a traditional word used to describe the operation of smoothing wood with abrasive paper, none of which is any longer made with sand. The abrasive paper is also often referred to colloquially as sandpaper.

Types of abrasive material

Of the various types of abrasive material used in different trades and industries the amateur furniture maker is concerned almost exclusively with glass, garnet and aluminium oxide. Silicon carbide and wire wool are occasionally used on hard lacquer finishes.

Glasspaper, with the exception of the 00 or flour grade, is a very inferior material for sanding hardwoods. It is relatively soft and the coarser grades, in particular, quickly lose their cutting surfaces. But flour grade glasspaper is a valuable material because it gives a smoother and finer finish then any other paper. Although the equivalent in grain size of 5/0 garnet paper, it gives the impression of being as fine, if not finer, than 9/0 garnet paper because it is much softer and does not bite so sharply into the wood.

Garnet paper, which is a reddish orange colour, is much harder than glass, cuts more quickly, and retains its cutting surface longer than glass.

Aluminium oxide, which is the same mineral as ruby, is tougher and harder than garnet. Woodworking aluminium oxide is usually a light sandy colour.

Silicon carbide is harder than aluminium oxide and is nearly as hard as diamond. It is familiar to many people as the black wet-and-dry paper used for rubbing down hard surfaces such as car bodies.

The 000 grade of wire wool is the finest of all the commonly used abrasive materials.

In addition to the abrasive material itself there are three other variables to be taken into account. These are grade or grit size, the density of the grit on the paper, and the thickness of the paper.

Grade or grit size

The most important of these three variables is grade or grit size which is a measure of the coarseness of the cutting surface. Different units of grading are used for each of the three types of paper and the equivalent grades are set out in Table I. The higher the number the finer is the grade (except for glass paper).

Density of grains

There are two patterns of grit on abrasive papers, open and closed. The grains on open-coat paper occupy about 50 per cent of the surface and on close-coat paper virtually all the surface. In theory,

Table 1

Common types of abrasive paper for woodworking

Aluminium oxide		Garnet		Glass	
grit size	backing paper	grade	backing paper	grade	backing paper
		9/0	A		
		8/0	A		
		7/0	A		
		6/0	A		
180	C	5/0	A C	00 (flour)	A
150	C	4/0	A C	0	A C
120	C	3/0	A C	1	C
100	C	2/0	A C	1½	C
80	C	0	A C	F2	C
60	C	½	C	M2	C
50	C	1	C	S2	C
40	C	1½	C	2½	C
36	C			3	C

The grit size of silicon carbide paper is classified in the same way as that of aluminium oxide.

the close-coat paper should cut more rapidly because it has more cutting edges, but in practice open-coat paper is more suitable for woodwork because it is less liable to clog.

Backing paper

Backing papers are of several thicknesses of which 'A' grade is the thinnest and, therefore, the most flexible. An 'A' grade paper should always be chosen for fine-grade finishing papers while the coarser papers for the preparatory work should have a 'C' grade backing. A 'D' grade is sometimes used for machine sanding-discs.

Sizes of abrasive papers

Most papers are available in a standard size of 280 mm by 230 mm (11 in by 9 in), but aluminium oxide and garnet papers are also available in a number of specialized sizes and shapes for powered sanding machines. A convenient size, which is sold in packets for small orbital sanders, is 235 mm by 94 mm (9¼ in by 3¾ in).

Use of abrasive papers

When the work has been cleaned and trimmed up after gluing, the surfaces are prepared for finishing by a series of sanding operations. It is both ineffective and a waste of effort to use a fine paper too soon and to jump from a coarse to a fine grade. The coarse paper makes relatively deep scratches

which the fine paper will not remove without a great deal of effort. The secret is to sand the work several times using a successively finer grade each time.

For almost all furniture work the preliminary cleaning and smoothing is best done with open-coat aluminium oxide paper having a C grade backing. The first sanding is done with a 60 or 80 grade paper followed successively with 100 and 120 grade paper. The later stages of sanding are better done with garnet paper varying from about 4/0 to 6/0 or 7/0 grade, and the final finish given with 00 grade glass paper.

Wood is cut down most quickly by sanding across the grain, but this makes deep scratches, especially with the coarser grades, and the sanding with each grade should be finished with the grain.

The paper is most conveniently wrapped round a wooden block for sanding. Some workers prefer to fix a wad of hard rubber or some other resilient material to the working surface of the block. This is said to make the paper last longer, but it is not really necessary, although very fine papers accumulate small, hard patches of wood dust which can mark the surface of the wood unless they are scraped off. These are less likely to occur if a more resilient sanding block is used.

Sanding always tends to wear away the sharp edges of wood, and the more resilient the sanding block the more likely is this to happen, as shown in figure 172a. It can be prevented by cramping pieces of waste wood along the edge of the work as in figure 172b.

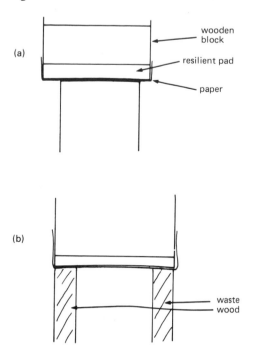

172   Sanding edges

Drawers and doors are first sanded independently of the surrounding frame but to ensure a perfectly flush fit, especially for curved drawers, they are then sanded, in situ, together with the bearer rails and the sides of the cabinet. When doing this, or more generally, when sanding any two pieces of wood which are joined at right angles, sanding across the grain is unavoidable.

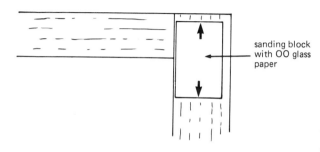

173   Sanding to remove cross-grain scratches

Provided a series of successively finer papers is used, the final stages of sanding with 6/0 or 7/0 garnet paper produces only superficial scratching, and this is removed by final sanding with the grain using 00 glass paper (figure 173).

Even open-coated paper is continually clogged with sawdust, but this can easily be removed by tapping the sanding block firmly against a hard surface.

Machine sanding

There are three types of sanding machine which can be operated with a small hand drill. these are disc sanders with a fixed spindle, disc sanders with a universal joint, and orbital sanders. Disc sanders with a fixed spindle are very liable to make deep grooves in the wood and are not suitable for fine work. Discs with a universal joint are less likely to cause damage, but even these have to be used with great care. Orbital sanders are safe but slow. After using all three types the author has come to the conclusion that the most satisfactory sequence is a finely set smoothing plane followed by a cabinet-maker's scraper, followed in turn by coarse and fine sanding by hand.

Finishing

Furniture is always treated with some form of finish to enhance the colour and figure of the wood and, usually, also to seal and protect the surface. Various waxes and oils were used until shellac-based french polish became popular in the early nineteenth century. Today, most factory-made furniture is finished with various forms of nitrocellulose, acid catalysed, polyester and polyurethane finishes. Most of these finishes are both unobtainable and impracticable for home use but various forms of polyurethane varnish, sometimes referred to as polyurethane lacquer, are particularly suitable.

There are five main types of finish which can be applied at home. These are wax, french polish, oil, varnish and amino resins. Before applying the finish it is occasionally desirable to fill or stain the wood.

Filling

A wood filler is used to fill the grain and sometimes, also, to stain the wood. It is only necessary when a very smooth finish is wanted on coarse-grained wood, and since it is usually desirable to retain the natural colour of the wood a transparent filler is normally used. It is applied after sanding and before waxing or varnishing. The filler itself, however, has to be sanded smooth before the final finish is put on.

Staining

Staining is not normally a recommended treatment for hand-made furniture, but it may occasionally be worthwhile staining light coloured pieces of wood if there is a pronounced variation in colour within a piece of furniture. Staining has to be done very carefully and it should first be tested on some small offcuts before being applied to a furniture component. The stain is applied after sanding.

Wax

Many people consider that the soft lustre of wax is the most beautiful of all wood finishes, but it gives no protection at all against heat and moisture, and a wet glass will leave a permanent stain which can only be removed by re-sanding the surface. Silicone waxes are said to be less vulnerable, but this is only a matter of degree, and no form of wax gives any real protection to the wood.

The recommended type of wax for new wood is beeswax dissolved in turpentine to give a consistency of soft butter. The author has used this and also various proprietary brands of furniture polish, and has been able to detect little or no difference between them. Whatever type of wax is used it is important to apply several coats and to buff the surface energetically with a soft duster.

Wax can also be applied over varnish with the advantage that stains will not penetrate to the wood. If the wax is marked it is easily cleaned off to the varnish layer with turpentine or white spirit and then replaced.

French polish

French polish is made of shellac and alcohol. The traditional method of application, which produces a very smooth, lustrous finish, is a highly skilled and somewhat esoteric art which the amateur is not advised to attempt unless he has had some instruction in the process. It is possible to buy shellac and alcohol preparations which are easy to apply, but they do not produce the very fine finish of the traditional method. No form of french polish is very resistant to heat or moisture.

Oil

Linseed oil, when rubbed into wood, slowly oxidizes to give a glossy and moderately protective coat. About a dozen applications spread over several months are required to give a substantial finish. Some more recent products, such as teak oil, incorporate an oxidizing agent, and these can be built up into an adequate coat with only two or three applications. No oil finish is very resistant to heat or moisture; it has to be renewed from time to time and gradually becomes rather sticky.

Varnish

Varnish is an omnibus term used to describe a range of products having very different chemical compositions and properties. The principal types are listed below in Table 2 in a very simplified and summary form. Of all the varnishes the most suitable for furniture are the polyurethane/alkyds or the polyurethanes. The polyurethanes, and especially the moisture-curing types, are technically the best, but may be difficult to obtain.

Amino resins

Amino resins are sold as butylated melamine or urea formaldehyde. They are obtainable in a one-pack or two-pack formulation and give a very hard surface which is resistant to heat and moisture. They do not darken with age.

Choice of finish

The most suitable finishes for home use are wax, one of the polyurethanes or an amino resin. Wax alone can be used on furniture which is not likely to be damaged by heat or moisture while formulations of matt polyurethane/alkyds, two-pack polyurethanes or amino resins give strong and resistant finishes which preserve the natural appearance of the wood. All polyurethanes, however, darken to some extent with age. Wax can be applied on top of a varnish or resin and if it is stained or marked it is easily removed from the finished surface with a solvent and replaced.

Polyurethane/alkyd varnish is easily obtained from most paint and hardware shops. Two-pack polyurethanes and amino resins are usually obtainable only from the more specialized shops. The moisture-curing polyurethanes are probably obtainable only from the manufacturers but owing to their toxicity and short shelf life they are not really suitable for home use.

Application of polyurethane varnish and amino resin

The varnish or resin is applied with a clean, fine brush in a dust-free atmosphere. Several coats are required and in order to obtain a good key either the successive coats have to be applied within less than a day of each other or the previous coat has to be rubbed down with fine aluminium oxide or silicon carbide paper. After the final coat has been sanded it is given a velvety finish by rubbing vigorously with 000 wire wool impregnated with wax polish. If a final coat of wax polish is required it is applied to the finished surface in the same way that it is put onto bare wood.

Table 2

Types and properties of varnish

Type	Properties
Oleo-resinous	Initially flexible but lose their flexibility with exposure. Relatively good exterior durability and water resistance. Tend to darken with age. Used on boats.
Alkyds	Good, general-purpose varnishes. Those based on soya oil are very pale in colour and do not darken with age. Those based on linseed oil do darken considerably. Durable and water resistant. Harden more slowly than polyurethanes. Obtainable in a glossy or matt formulation.
Polyurethane/alkyds (air drying formulation)	A one-pack chemical formulation of alkyd and polyurethane varnishes. Harder and more heat and moisture resistant than oleo-resinous or alkyd varnishes but tend to discolour. Less durable out of doors than alkyds. Harden rapidly. Obtainable in a glossy or matt formulation.
Polyurethanes (two-pack formulation)	Very hard and very resistant to heat and moisture. Vary in their flexibility and colour retention. Less durable out of doors than alkyds. Obtainable in a glossy or matt formulation. Short pot life.
Polyurethane (one-pack moisture-curing formulation)	Very hard and resistant to heat and moisture. Good durability. Good colour retention. Less durable out of doors than alkyds. Obtainable in a glossy or matt formulation. Short shelf life. Toxic and relatively slow drying, especially in warm dry conditions.

Definition

Utility furniture in the context of this chapter is assumed to mean furniture or fittings made of relatively inexpensive softwood or wood-based materials which are either painted or surfaced with a sheet material such as melamine-faced film. The furniture may be either free standing or fitted to the fabric of the house.

The methods and materials used in making utility furniture are usually quite different from those used in cabinet making with which this book is primarily concerned. But since many amateur woodworkers develop their basic woodworking skills in making various types of utility furniture for the house, some general information is given in this chapter on the materials and techniques used in this type of work. For detailed guidance on the design and construction of utility furniture and higher quality fitted furniture the reader should refer to books on joinery.

The appearance of utility furniture depends almost entirely upon its design and the quality of its painted or faced surfaces and hardly at all upon the decorative value of its structural materials and constructional details. Its strength often relies to a large extent upon the structure to which it is fitted. The traditional high quality and expensive furniture timbers are therefore quite inappropriate for this type of work, and the carefully cut joints and precise workmanship of the cabinet maker are rarely necessary. On the other hand an understanding of the appropriate techniques and an appreciation of the properties of the materials used are required. Accurate measuring, marking and cutting are also necessary for successful results.

Materials

The materials used in making utility furniture are softwood timber, plywood, blockboard, laminboard, particle board and hardboard. All the man-made sheet materials are also available in a wide range of decorated and surfaced forms.

Softwood

The most inexpensive timber is usually a softwood. The species is of little importance for most purposes but the wood should be well seasoned, straight grained and free from large knots and other defects such as reaction wood (page 13). Ring width is not critical but wood with fewer than about six rings to 25 mm (1 in) is likely to be weaker and to give a poorer painted finish than wood with narrower rings.

Particle board

Particle board, or chipboard, is made of small, graded wood chips mixed with an adhesive, usually urea formaldehyde, and pressed into flat sheets. The normal thicknesses are 3.2 mm ($\frac{1}{8}$ in), 4 mm ($\frac{3}{16}$ in), 6 mm ($\frac{1}{4}$ in), 9 mm ($\frac{3}{8}$ in), 12 mm ($\frac{1}{2}$ in), 15 mm ($\frac{9}{16}$ in), 16 mm ($\frac{5}{8}$ in), 18 mm ($\frac{3}{4}$ in), 22 mm ($\frac{7}{8}$ in), 25 mm (1 in), and 30 mm ($1\frac{1}{8}$ in).

Single layer particle board is homogeneous in structure, three layer board has finer and denser surfaces with a coarse core, while graded-density board has a fine texture on the surfaces which becomes progressively coarser towards the centre. The individual chips are aligned in all directions but predominantly in the same plane as the surface of the board.

Particle board is denser than most woods but its modulus of rupture, which is the same in all directions, is much less than that of comparable plywood, blockboard or wood (parallel with the grain).

It is relatively stable in the plane of the board but expands appreciably in thickness with increase in moisture content and if subjected continually to high humidity it tends to lose its structure. If one side of the board is veneered it is liable to bow with changes in moisture content and unless it is held rigidly in position a backing veneer is needed to maintain stability.

Particle board is rather crumbly to work but it can be sawn, planed on the edge, bored and sanded. It cannot satisfactorily be planed to thickness and it does not hold nails or screws well, especially on the edges. There are, however, special particle board screws which hold relatively strongly. Cutting tools are quickly blunted by the hard urea formaldehyde adhesive.

Particle board in the thicker dimensions is quite rigid in short lengths and is used structurally in various forms of utility furniture. It has very good gluing characteristics and, having no end grain, a strong edge-to-edge or face joint can be made with glue alone. The face should be lightly sanded before gluing to remove the surface glaze. Current and future research is likely to produce improved forms of particle board having greater strength and better weathering properties than the present products.

Hardboard

There are three principal types of fibre board of which hardboard is one. The other two are insulation board and wall board neither of which is used in furniture making. Hardboard is made by subjecting wood fibres to steam heat and pressure to form a dark brown, dense, sheet material. No glue is used in the process, but a water repellent such as size is usually added, and sometimes also phenol formaldehyde to give added strength. The fibres are usually wet-pressed against a mesh and this gives the characteristic texture on the reverse side of the sheet. Some hardboard, known as duoboard, is made from dry fibres for which a mesh is unnecessary and the board is consequently smooth on both sides. The normal thicknesses of standard hardboard are 3.2 mm ($\frac{1}{8}$ in), 4.8 mm ($\frac{3}{16}$ in), and 6.4 mm ($\frac{1}{4}$ in).

There are three broad categories of hardboard. Medium board is the weakest and is less dense than particle board. Standard board is the most widely used and is denser than particle board whilst tempered board is the densest and strongest and is also the most resistant to moisture.

Hardboard is very stable and can be planed on the edges, sawn, drilled and sanded. It is rather woolly to work and should be sawn from the face side because it tends to tear away from the lower surface. For this reason it also needs to be supported close to the saw cut.

Hardboard is flexible and is used almost exclusively as a panel material supported on a wooden frame. Like particle board, the surface should be sanded lightly before gluing.

Plywood

Plywood is made by gluing an odd number of wood veneers from a wide variety of hardwood and softwood timber in alternate directions, usually at right angles to each other. Most internal plywood is bonded with urea formaldehyde and external, or marine, grades with phenol formaldehyde. Marine plywood is about double the price of internal plywood of the same thickness.

Apart from some very thin and specialized plywood the usual thicknesses are 3 mm ($\frac{1}{8}$ in), 4

mm, 5 mm, 6 mm, 6.5 mm ($\frac{1}{4}$ in), 8 mm, 9 mm, 9.5 mm ($\frac{3}{8}$ in), 12 mm, 12.5 mm ($\frac{1}{2}$ in), 15 mm, 16 mm ($\frac{5}{8}$ in), 17.5 mm, 18 mm, 19 mm ($\frac{3}{4}$ in), 21 mm, 22 mm ($\frac{7}{8}$ in), 24 mm, 25 mm (1 in), and 25.5 mm.

Plywood has a greater strength to weight ratio than steel and is almost as strong laterally as longitudinally. It is stable, does not split, and holds nails and screws well especially in the surface grain. The larger the number of plies the greater is the stability. Plywood tends to tear away on the lower surface when sawn but this can be prevented by scoring a line with a marking knife and sawing just outside it. Thick plywood can be jointed like solid wood.

Blockboard and laminboard

Blockboard and laminboard consist of a core of wooden strips of equal thickness and width laid longitudinally, glued edge to edge and sandwiched between two or four sheets of veneer. The individual strips of blockboard are about 25 mm (1 in) wide and of laminboard about 7 mm ($\frac{5}{16}$ in) wide. Laminboard, having more glue, is stronger and denser than blockboard. The usual thicknesses of blockboard and laminboard are 12 mm ($\frac{1}{2}$ in), 13 mm, 16 mm, 18 mm, 19 mm ($\frac{3}{4}$ in), 22 mm, 25 mm (1 in), 32 mm. and 38 mm ($1\frac{1}{2}$ in).

Blockboard and laminboard have properties similar to those of a solid conifer board but they are more stable, particularly across the grain. They can be jointed, although not very elegantly, and they hold screws strongly in the surfaces and edges. They are therefore suitable for flush doors and as a base for working surfaces but, when painted, the longitudinal pattern of the core material tends to show through the three-ply boards which have only one layer of wood veneer on each surface.

Melamine sheet material

Melamine sheet consists of a thin film of melamine bonded to several sheets of resin-bonded kraft paper. It forms a clean, hard decorative or working surface when bonded to a base material such as particle board, hardboard or blockboard. When melamine sheet material is veneered to a base material in the factory it is usully glued with urea formaldehyde in a press and the resulting bond is extremely strong. When it is bonded in situ rubber impact glue is almost always used and this gives a considerably weaker bond.

Melamine can be sawn, planed and filed but it quickly blunts cutting edges. It tends to chip when sawn but this can be avoided by scoring a line with a marking knife before sawing.

It is easily glued into position by following the directions given with the adhesive. The top sheet is applied first and this should overlap the edge by a little more than the thickness of the lipping strip (figure 174a). The lipping strip is planed to a straight edge on each side and to the correct width and glued into position against the underside of the top sheet (figure 174b). The projecting edge of the top sheet is planed almost flush with the lip and then finally trimmed to the lip and given a slight bevel with a file (figure 174c).

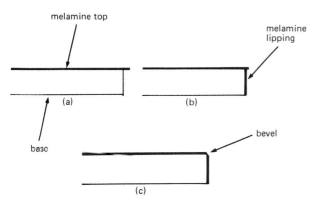

174   Gluing melamine sheet in situ

Thicknesses of panel products in the USA
Panel products are still sold on the retail market in the USA in imperial units. The most common thicknesses are $\frac{1}{8}$ in, $\frac{3}{16}$ in, $\frac{1}{4}$ in, $\frac{5}{16}$ in, $\frac{3}{8}$ in, $\frac{1}{2}$ in, $\frac{5}{8}$ in, $\frac{3}{4}$ in, and 1 in.

The choice of material
Panel materials
There are three panel materials. These are plywood, hardboard and particle board. It will be seen from Table 3 that hardboard and particle board of comparable thickness are approximately the same price while plywood is about twice as expensive. All are stable and easy to work and plywood is only justified where additional strength is required.
Structural materials
The choice lies between softwood, thick plywood, thick particle board, blockboard or laminboard. Of these, laminboard is more than four times as expensive as particle board, while plywood and blockboard are roughly three times the cost. For most types of framing, softwood is the most versatile as well as being one of the cheapest materials. Blockboard is useful for simple, unframed doors and particle board as a base material for working surfaces where strength is not important. For shelving, softwood combines strength with reasonable economy and since it does not require lipping the additional work of planing to size and finishing does not prevent it being the best choice for most purposes.

Table 3
The properties of panel and structural materials

Panel materials	Stability*		Strength	Relative price per unit area (18 mm softwood = 100)
	Longitudinal	Transverse		
Plywood (3 mm)	0.13	0.15	xxxx	40
Hardboard (3.2 mm)	0.23	0.25	xx	20
Particle board (3.2 mm)	0.31	0.32	xx	20
Structural materials (18 mm)				
Softwood	0.15	2.50	xxx	100
Plywood	0.13	0.14	xxxxx	175
Particle board	0.31	0.32	xx	60
Blockboard	0.21	0.13	xxx	150
Laminboard	0.19	0.09	xxxx	275

*percentage movement for a change in relative humidity from 35 per cent to 85 per cent.

The properties of the various materials are summarised in Table 3 but it is not possible to make precise comparisons of cost, strength or stability between the various materials. There are considerable variations within each type, and the characteristics as well as the absolute values of strength and stability vary from material to material.

Strength, in particular, is extremely difficult to compare because there is such a wide range within each material that the values of one material overlap those of another. Table 3 is, therefore, intended to be only a very general guide, and the strength ratings are derived from a purely subjective assessment.

Painting
Wood
The surface is rubbed down with successively finer abrasive paper and any knots or resin pockets painted with knotting to prevent subsequent resin exudation. Any surface imperfections are filled with a cellulose filler, which is rubbed down with fine abrasive paper when dry. If the wood is to be painted with an oil-bound paint, a wood primer is applied first, followed by one or two undercoats before the top coat. The surface should be lightly sanded between each coat with fine abrasive paper. Emulsion paint can be applied both as a primer and an undercoat if it is also to be used as a top coat.

Particle board
Particle board can be sanded to bring the margins or edges flush with adjoining members, but the surface should not otherwise be sanded. A filler is always required unless the texture of the board is to be retained for decorative purposes. After the filler has been rubbed down the particle board is treated in the same way as wood.

Hardboard
Hardboard can be sanded in the same way as particle board but the surface should not unnecessarily be roughened. Before painting with an oil-bound paint, hardboard should be prepared with a hardboard primer. It is otherwise treated in the same way as wood or particle board.

Plywood
The grain in the plywood is first filled with a cellulose filler, after which it is given the same treatment as wood. For some purposes even moderate quality plywood may be varnished instead of painted, in which case it should first be lightly sanded with fine abrasive paper.

Methods of construction
Wood framing
The basic structure for fitted cupboards is a frame with rails morticed into stiles at the top and bottom (figure 175a). For double doors a central stile may be added (figure 175b), and for two-tiered cupboards a third rail is required (figure 175c), which is morticed into the side stiles and fitted to the central stile with a cross-halving joint (figure 99).

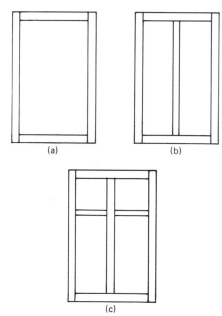

175   Wood framing

If the cupboard is fitted into an alcove no other structure is required apart from wall battens for holding the framework and internal shelving. If the cupboard is fitted into a corner a side frame is morticed into one of the stiles, as in figure 176.

For a free-standing cabinet, the construction is basically the same as that of a table, but with rails at the bottom as well as at the top of the legs. It is possible to make a free-standing or corner cupboard without using any joints at all other than those required for the framework of the door. Side and back panels are made by gluing a sheet material, such as hardboard, on to an unjointed wooden framework (figure 177a). The sheet material of the side panels overlaps the framework so that the three panels together with the door frame can be assembled merely by screwing the framework together, as in figure 177b, and gluing the overlapping sheet material to the wooden uprights.

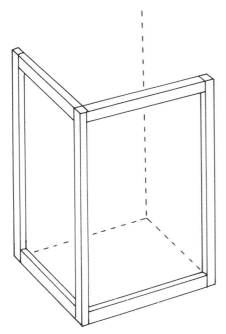

176   Corner frame

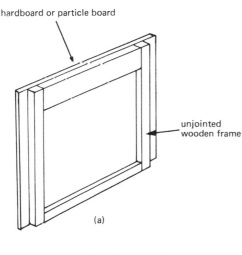

hardboard or particle board

unjointed
wooden frame

(a)

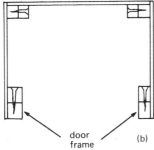

door
frame

(b)

177   Hardboard panels

Working tops
A rigid top of plywood, particle board or blockboard can be screwed and glued to the rails of the frame, and then lipped and painted or faced and edged with melamine. The top can alternatively be held with buttons (page 77).

Fixing panels
There are several ways of fixing panels to a wooden framework apart from the method described in the previous paragraph. The frame can be rebated, as in figure 178a, or artificially rebated, as in figure 178b, by fixing a fillet of wood to the side of the frame.

The panel can partly overlap the frame leaving a space to be filled with a fillet, as in figure 178c, or wholly overlap the frame, as in figure 178d. In methods 'c' and 'd' the edge can either be sanded flush with the frame and the edge filled with cellulose filler before painting, or the join can be covered with a hollow-square moulding, as in figure 178d.

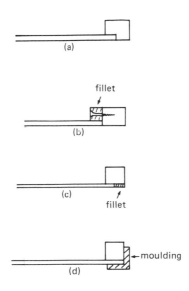

(a)

fillet

(b)

(c)

fillet

moulding

(d)

178   Fixing panels to a frame

If the frame is large, some cross supports are needed to keep the panel rigid. These are morticed into the uprights.

The panels of hardboard, plywood or particle board can be held with panel pins alone, especially with fitted furniture which does not rely upon the panels for its strength and rigidity. For free-standing furniture, especially with unjointed frames, the panels should be pinned and glued to give additional strength.

Fixing to walls

Walls are rarely flat or perpendicular, and corners of rooms are rarely at right angles. Before fixing the rectangular frame of a fitted cupboard into the corner of a room, the front and the side components should each be held vertically against the wall and the contours of the wall marked onto the frame. This is done by holding a pencil against a block of wood which is as wide as the largest gap between the frame and the wall (figure 179a), and running the block of wood down the wall (figure 179c). The frame is then planed and cut with a spokeshave to the pencil line.

When the frame has been shaped to the wall it is held vertically in position and a pencil line drawn onto the wall against the inside of the frame. A batten has to be fixed onto the wall against this line and the frame screwed to the batten. A builder usually nails the batten into position with cut nails, but the amateur is not advised to do this because there is a good chance of ending up with a loose batten and broken plaster. The best method is to screw the batten into position.

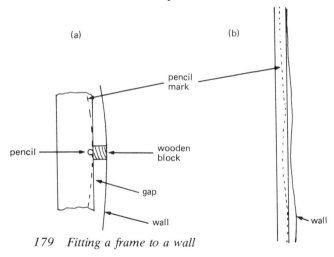

179   Fitting a frame to a wall

Screw holes are drilled in the batten, screws inserted into the holes so that they just protrude from the other side, and, with the batten held in the correct position, each screw is lightly tapped with a hammer to mark the positions for drilling holes. These can easily be drilled into breeze-block wall with a hand drill fitted with a masonry drill. Brick walls are very much more difficult and usually require a masonry punch, which is twisted with one hand as it is hammered with the other. The punch is used alternately with the drill.

Very often the holes are slightly out of position when they have been drilled, with the result that the batten is not correctly aligned on the wall when it is screwed home. This problem, however, is solved very easily. After plugging the holes with fibre or plastic plugs to take the screws, the batten is held in the correct position and nailed to the wall with masonry pins. These are very hard, strong nails which will penetrate masonry quite easily, and although they are not strong enough for permanent fixing they will hold the batten firmly in place while the screws are screwed in. Any slight discrepancy in alignment is taken up by the plastic plugs and not by movement of the batten.

The same method is used when fixing horizontal supports for shelving.

Mouldings

It is virtually impossible to achieve a perfect fit between a frame and the wall, and a moulding serves the double purpose of hiding the gap and providing a decorative finish to the work. Mouldings of various shapes and sizes can be bought from timber merchants. A moulding is more easily painted before than after fixing, and it can be pushed firmly against the contours of the wall as it is tacked into position on the frame with panel pins which are punched into the wood. The punch holes and any gaps between the moulding and the frame are filled with cellulose filler and the paintwork re-touched.

Doors

Figure 43 shows an example of utility furniture made of painted softwood and constructed by traditional methods. But whereas solid wooden door panels have to be free to move within the frames, stable materials like plywood and hardboard do not. They can be used as structural members and glued to a jointed or unjointed frame.

Figure 180a shows a cross section through a simple door made by tacking and gluing thin panels onto either side of an unjointed softwood frame, the stiles and rails being held in position only by the panels. A neater finish is obtained if a thin fillet of wood is glued to each edge, as in figure 180b. A large door made in this way requires some internal support such as additional rails, but a wooden distance piece glued into position is sufficient for a small door (figure 180b).

Thicker sheets of blockboard or laminboard can be used as solid doors. Plywood and especially particle board are less satisfactory because they have the two disadvantages of being relatively heavy materials and of not holding screws very strongly in the edge grain.

If there are two doors to a cupboard or cabinet

they can be made to close edge to edge, as in figure 180c, or to overlap, as in figure 180d (page 86). It is not satisfactory to cut a rebate into a panel material, but false rebates can be made by tacking and gluing fillets of wood to the edges of the doors, as in figure 180d.

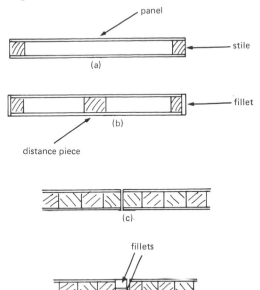

180   *Construction of unjointed doors*

Sliding doors are often required in kitchen cabinets. A number of proprietary fittings are available to give a smooth sliding action, but there are two simple methods which can be used in utility furniture. In the first method grooves are cut into the top and bottom of the carcase and hardwood tongues tacked or screwed and glued onto the top and bottom of each door to slide in the grooves. The tongue and groove at the top are deeper than those at the bottom so that the door may be lifted

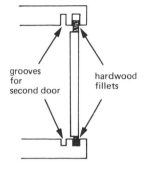

181   *Sliding doors*

into the top groove and then dropped into the bottom one without disengaging from the top (figure 181), The second method is simply the reverse of the first one. The grooves are cut into the door rails and the hardwood tongues glued into channels cut into the carcase.

Drawers

In place of the dovetails used in traditionally constructed furniture, the sides of drawers made of particle board or plywood can be butt jointed, with or without a stopped housing, into the drawer front (figure 182a). The back is similarly butt jointed and nailed to the sides. The nails are used here to position the back rather than to provide strength. With this form of construction the door front overlaps the front of the cabinet and an imperfect fit cannot be seen, although it can be felt when the drawer is pulled in and out (figure 182b).

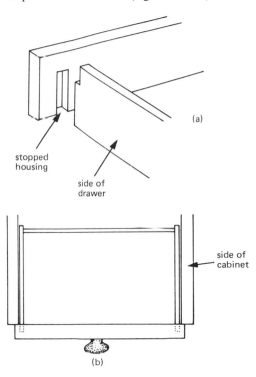

182   *Utility drawers*

Softwood furniture

Softwood timber and traditional methods of construction can be used to make utility furniture, such as the fitted cabinet and bookcase shown in figure 43. Less precision is needed in this type of work than in hardwood cabinet making because no one, except the maker, sees the joints which are filled and painted, although they have to be accurate enough to prevent distortion and to provide adequate strength. But the amateur furniture maker is well advised to work as accurately as possible, no matter what type of work he is doing, because the construction of utility furniture provides an opportunity of improving his skill and experience.

CHAPTER 19 **Metal fittings**

The metal fittings likely to be used by the amateur furniture maker are screws, hinges, door, drawer and box locks, key escutcheons, door fastenings, door and drawer handles and, possibly, brass corners, such as those on the chest which is illustrated in figure 45. Despite its higher price, brass is almost always used in preference to steel because it looks very much better and does not rust. On the other hand, steel fittings are often suitable for utility furniture.

Screws
With the exception of key escutcheons, all the fittings mentioned above, plus drawer runners, table-top buttons, and the backs of carcases, are fixed to the wood with screws of which there are three principal types as illustrated in figure 183.

The larger the gauge the stronger the screw, and a screw with a given gauge has the same thickness of shank no matter how long it is. All the screws illustrated in figure 183 have conventionally slotted heads. There are, in addition, various types of star-shaped slot which require special screw drivers, and which are more expensive but easier to screw.

The hole for the shank should be the same diameter as the widest part of the shank and the hole for the thread should be the diameter of the central core of the thread. It is, therefore, only the thread itself which grips the wood. Since the thread is tapered, it is advisable to drill two holes for a long screw, as shown in figure 184, especially if it is of a high gauge, in which case it will have a pronounced taper.

For a countersunk screw the hole has to be countersunk with a countersink bit.

Brass screws are much weaker than steel screws, and it is easy to screw the shank off the thread of a small-gauge brass screw. This is very awkward in a hinge or lock, and to reduce the risk of it happening it is advisable to screw a steel screw, of the same size, fully into the hole and then to remove it before inserting the brass screw.

184   *Drilling screw holes*

Hinges
The only type of hinge commonly used in furniture making is a plain butt hinge which is narrow enough to be let into the thickness of a door.
Fitting
Two hinges, fitted about one tenth to one twelfth of the height of the door from the top and bottom edges, are adequate for most cabinet doors. They should be narrower than the width of the door and recessed an equal distance into the side of the door and the side of the cabinet. The depth of each recess is a fraction less than half the thickness of the hinge when the two arms are parallel with each other (figure 185).

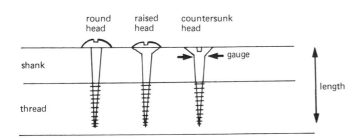

183   *Types of screw*

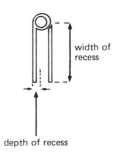

185   *Fitting hinges*

The hinges are fitted first to the door and then to the cabinet. The position of each hinge is marked approximately with a pencil an equal distance from the top and bottom of each door. The depth of the recess is measured directly from the hinge with a cutting gauge set with the flat edge of the blade outwards and marked between the pencil lines. The width of the hinge is measured and marked with a cutting gauge so that the central axis of the hinge just projects in front of the door (figure 185). The length is then accurately marked with a try square and marking knife so that the hinge will fit tightly into the recess. The waste is removed with a chisel and finished with a router plane used in the same way as in truing a tenon (page 58).

Before drilling the screw holes, the hinge is pushed firmly into the recess and the centre of each hole is marked with a sharp awl to make sure that the drill will be correctly centred. Sometimes the screw heads are larger than the countersunk holes in the hinge. If this is so, the brass is easily drilled deeper with a countersink drill. When the hinges have been screwed into the recess, the door is placed in the open position with the bottom edge resting on a thin piece of card or abrasive (flour) paper and the position of the hinges marked on the side of the cabinet. The recesses are then marked and cut in the same way as in the door. The setting of the cutting gauge for the width of the recess should remain unchanged to ensure that the front of the door is exactly flush with the front of the cabinet. If by any mischance the hinge is wrongly positioned, the mistake can be rectified (page 130).

Locks
Drawer locks
Locks are most easily recessed into the drawer front before the drawer is assembled. A normal drawer lock and the recess which is cut into the inside of the drawer are shown in figure 186a and b.

The length of the lock is marked with a pencil, symmetrically on either side of the mid point of the drawer front, lines AEC and BFD in figure 186b. The width and depth, AE and EC, are measured directly from the lock with a cutting gauge and marked between the pencil lines. The length is then measured on the wood directly from the lock and the lines AEC and BFD re-marked with a try square and marking knife. The thickness of the outer plate of the lock is then marked on the edge and the inside face of the drawer, and the wood cut down to the lines with a chisel and router plane, as in figure 186b. The deeper recess for the body of

the lock is marked within the shallow recess, as shown by the dotted lines in figure 186b and the waste wood removed with a chisel and router plane. The lock is pushed home into the recess as far as it will go making an indentation, shown as a dotted circle in figure 186b, where the key spindle protrudes. This indentation marks the centre of the keyhole. A small block of wood is cramped to the front of the drawer opposite the indentation to prevent the wood splitting, and a hole, just large enough for the key spindle, is bored exactly at right angles through the indentation. It is now possible to push the lock into its recess and to check that the hole for the key spindle is in precisely the right position. If it is not, it is enlarged with a small round file, so that its centre is correctly located. The lock is not screwed into position until the keyhole has been cut and the escutcheon fitted (page 127).

When the drawer has finally been fitted into the finished cabinet, a recess has to be cut into the underside of the bearer rail to take the bolt of the lock. The position of the recess is marked by smearing the face of the bolt with paint and turning the key towards the locked position. The shape and position of the bolt is then imprinted with paint on the rail. The cabinet is turned upside down to cut the recess and the rail made rigid by wedging a block of wood between it and the next rail. Since the space between the rails is restricted, a drawer lock chisel may be needed for this job.

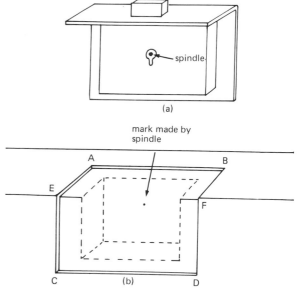

186   *Drawer lock and recess*

Although a simple recess is acceptable, it is preferable to countersink a brass plate with a slot cut through it equal in size to the bolt of the lock. This is positioned over the recess, and any final adjustment made by filing the slot as necessary.

An alternative method is to position as carefully as possible and cut the recesses for the bolt and brass plate before gluing up the carcase. Any final adjustment is then made when the drawer is fitted.

Box locks

The body of a box lock is fitted in exactly the same way as a drawer lock, but instead of a rectangular bolt there are two catches which slide into two small housings projecting from the upper plate. To locate the plate on the lid of the box, the catches are engaged in their housings, and the lid pushed against the plate. There are usually two small projections on the plate which will make indentations in the lid. If these are absent the plate is smeared with paint which leaves a mark on the lid. The plate is recessed flush with the wood and screwed into position.

Door locks

A cut door lock is almost exactly the same as a drawer lock and is marked and fitted in the same way. Since the bolt shoots in only one direction a left or right-handed lock has to be used according to the position of the hinges.

A straight cupboard lock, which is more suitable for fitted furniture, is not recessed but is screwed directly onto the inside of the door. The bolts usually shoot right or left so the lock can be fitted on either a right or left-handed door.

Key escutcheons

A keyhole is usually lined with a brass escutcheon and the hole has to be cut so that the escutcheon fits tightly into it. This is done by boring two holes, as shown in figure 187.

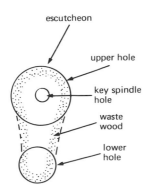

187   Fitting keyhole escutcheons

The upper hole is centred on the key spindle hole, which is already drilled, and its diameter is equal to the diameter of the circular portion of the escutcheon. The diameter of the lower hole is equal to the width of the tail of the escutcheon. These two holes are bored from the front of the drawer and the intervening wood, which is indicated by dotted lines in figure 187, is removed with a keyhole saw and file. The precise position of the lower hole can be clearly marked by placing the escutcheon in its correct position in relation to the key-spindle hole and giving it a tap with a hammer, thus marking its shape in the wood. The lock is screwed into position and the escutcheon tapped into its recess with a hammer against a small block of hardwood, which protects the drawer front.

Door fastenings

Apart from locks there are three main types of door fastening: sliding bolts, spring catches and magnetic catches. It is always preferable to fit fastenings at the top and bottom of the door to prevent any tendency to warp.

Sliding bolts

Sliding bolts are often fixed to the doors of fitted cupboards but more rarely to articles of furniture. They are not usually recessed but some are let into the edge of the door.

Spring catches

Spring catches are not recommended for cabinet doors because their action tends to be rather harsh.

Magnetic catches

Magnetic catches are the most suitable form of door fastening because they are positive but smooth in their action. A metal plate has generally to be recessed into the corner of the door so that it is flush with the inner surface.

Handles and knobs

There are many types of door and drawer handles and knobs but there is little to say about them because they are easy to fit and their choice is a matter of personal preference.

It is, however, important to make sure that knobs and handles are correctly positioned. A combination square is a useful tool for this job. It can be set to measure the distance of handles from the end and also from the top of each drawer. The position of each screw or bolt hole is marked with a sharp awl before drilling the hole.

Brass chest corners

Brass chest corners are fitted to military chests and occasionally to boxes and table tops. They are recessed so that their surfaces are flush with the surface of the wood. The shape of the recess cannot directly be marked from the brass corner, because the thickness of the metal prevents it from being correctly located on any of the three surfaces. Before marking, any protrusions on the inside of the corner should be filed off. The corner is held firmly in position on the corner of the chest, and its outline AB, in figure 188a, marked on the top surface with the point of a marking knife. The thickness of the metal is marked along the two edges and the waste wood removed from the top with a small chisel and router plane, thus allowing the corner to lie flush with the top of the chest (figure 188b).

The final position of the lower edge of the brass corner can then be marked on the wood, and the waste removed in the same way as from the top. When the two edges have been recessed, each has to be extended by the thickness of the metal, as indicated by the shaded area A in figure 188b. The corner can then be fully recessed along the two edges and the final position, shown by a dotted line in figure 188b, marked on the top surface. This is removed with a small chisel and router and the corner screwed into position.

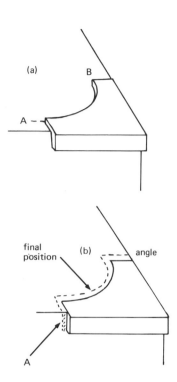

188   Fitting brass corners

CHAPTER 20

Mistakes and maintenance

Avoiding mistakes

The amateur worker inevitably makes mistakes, partly because he is inexperienced, but mainly because he has to work sporadically. Each time he continues a job, he is liable to have forgotten precisely what he was doing or intending to do when he stopped working on the previous occasion. It is important, therefore, to be as methodical as possible and, in particular, to mark the various components of a piece of furniture clearly with a pencil.

Marking

As each piece of wood is earmarked for a particular function and cut approximately to size, it should be identified with a distinguishing mark, and before any piece of wood is cut it should be checked to see whether it carries such a mark. At this stage the marks need not identify the precise location of the piece but only, for example, that it is a leg, a rail or a stile.

When all the components have been planed true and are ready for jointing each piece should be numbered or lettered with reference to a plan because hand-cut joints are not interchangeable and the matching pairs have to be clearly identified. Care is needed not to lose the identity of a piece of wood by scraping or sanding off its distinguishing mark. To avoid this happening, the marks can be transferred from the face of the wood to the joints, but the mark should be replaced on the face of the wood before gluing because a pencil mark is easily obscured by the glue.

Correcting mistakes

Many mistakes can be repaired perfectly well but a line has to be drawn between acceptable repairs and sloppy workmanship. One should be prepared, when necessary, to reject a faulty piece of work and to do the job again. A few of the more common mistakes and ways of correcting them are listed below.

Faulty cutting

A piece of wood may be cut too short or too narrow or planed too thin. It is not usually practicable to lengthen a furniture component because the joint would be unsightly, but this is of no importance if the wood is to be painted and two pieces of wood can easily be joined longitudinally with some form of scarf joint which does not greatly weaken the member. Two such types are shown in figure 189.

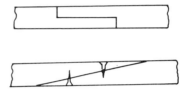

189 Scarf joints

There are no problems from the point of view of strength or appearance in gluing an edge strip to increase the width or a thick veneer to increase the thickness of a piece of wood.

Surface defects

Surface defects are more likely to be due to natural faults than to mistakes in workmanship, but whatever the cause they can often be repaired. Small knots or holes are drilled out and plugged with a small piece of similar wood having a matching grain. A circular plug is marked out with a pair of dividers and cut out with a chisel. The plug is glued into position and left a little proud of the surface. When the glue has set the projecting portion is planed off and sanded. A larger defect is cut out and patched in the same way that a chess square is set into a board. It is a matter of opinion whether a patch should appear on the external surface of a piece of furniture, but provided it is neatly done and is not very conspicuous, it is probably an acceptable feature of hand-made work.

Faulty joints

The most common faults are to cut mortices too wide, to split mortices by forcing in tenons which are too thick, and to split the outside pins of dovetail joints by forcing in tails which are too wide.

If, after truing a mortice-and-tenon joint, the tenon is found to be too thin, a thick shaving of wood is cut with a coarsely-set plane and glued to whichever cheek of the tenon needs building up.

A split mortice is forced open, glue spread on each surface with a fine sliver of wood and the two split surfaces cramped together. The tenon is shaved down to the correct thickness and fitted into the mortice when the glue has set and with the cramp still in position. When the joint has finally been assembled and glued the tenon holds the mortice firmly together and there is no loss in strength as a result of the split. The same method is used if the outer pins of a dovetail are split.

If the tails do not fit accurately into the pins of a dovetail joint there is no satisfactory solution if the joint is a visual feature of the work. But if the dovetail is not visible, thin slivers of wood can be gently tapped and glued into the gaps to make the joint strong, even if inelegant.

The author on one occasion cut the pins on the back of a drawer from the wrong side but was able, nevertheless, to make a strong, rigid joint by re-marking and cutting from the correct side and filling the gaps with wedges. This is a good example, incidentally, of what happens if the pieces of wood are not correctly identified.

If a mortice is incorrectly positioned or is cut longer than the width of the tenon, the joint may fit tightly, but the edges of the two components may not be flush with each other. A very small discrepancy is easily corrected but a larger one is more difficult. If, for example, a bookshelf, after it

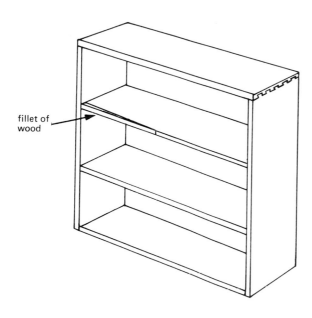

190 Correcting inset bookshelf

fillet of wood

has been glued, is inset instead of being flush with the edges of the bookcase, there are two ways of correcting the fault. One is to plane all the edges of the bookcase and the other shelves back to the level of the wrongly positioned shelf. The other is to glue a thin fillet of matching wood to the front of the shelf, as shown in figure 190.

Failure to stop grooves and rebates
Probably the most common fault is to cut a panel groove through to the end of a door stile which is jointed to the rail with a simple mortice-and-tenon joint. This is not a very serious mistake because the small channels at the top and bottom of the door are easily plugged with wooden fillets. An unstopped rebate is likely to be more serious because it usually occurs on the inside surface of a door or in the side of a cabinet (page 83). There is no difficulty in patching a groove with a piece of wood but this is more like bad workmanship than acceptable repair work.

Faulty positioning of hinges
It sometimes happens that the holes for a hinge are not drilled in exactly the right position. The error can only be in one direction because the recess prevents movement in the other three directions. If the error is in the cabinet, the effect is to set the door too far forwards, while if it is in the stile the door is set too far back. The error is easily remedied by gluing wooden plugs into the holes and re-drilling them in their correct positions. The plug should be of approximately the same hardness as the surrounding wood, otherwise the drill is liable to wander off centre as the hole is being drilled.

If the hinge recess is made slightly too deep a piece of flour (abrasive) paper can be cut to size and fitted between the hinge and the wood without affecting the grip of the screws. If a larger correction is necessary, after the screw holes have been drilled, the holes have to be plugged and a thin wooden distance piece glued in the recess before the holes are re-drilled. Provided the distance piece does not exceed about 1 mm ($\frac{1}{32}$ in) in thickness, and is chosen to match the grain of the wood, it is almost entirely obscured by the projection of the hinge.

Maintenance

Unsupported or partially supported furniture components such as doors and drawers sometimes distort slightly in service, even if they were made with well-seasoned wood. A door is partly constrained by catches at the top and bottom, but these do not always prevent twisting, and if the front of a drawer has a tendency to twist, the back and sides are not sufficiently robust to restrain it. These faults can often be corrected or ameliorated but it is not advisable to do anything until after the wood has been in service for about a year and has reached a state of approximate equilibrium.

The surface of wood is often scratched or damaged by heat or a spilled liquid. This form of damage can usually be repaired, the method depending upon the type of finish (page 114).

Doors

There are two ways of truing a slightly twisted door. One method is to bend it in the opposite direction as described in Chapter 1 (page 15) for straightening a twisted board. This is a somewhat imprecise method and a more accurate way is to plane off the portion of the door frame which is projecting beyond the frame of the cabinet. The thickness of wood to be removed is unlikely to be more than about 1.5 mm ($\frac{1}{16}$ in) from a hardwood cabinet door, and the reduction in thickness of the door is much less obvious than the distortion.

Drawers

If the front of a drawer twists it is not only seen to be out of true but may also cause the sides to stick when it is slid in and out. The first thing is to check the drawer for wind, and to plane the bottom edge of the side which is twisted downwards parallel with the bottom edge of the other side. This will centralize the drawer front in its opening, and will probably prevent sticking. If the drawer still sticks, the cause is likely to be the top edge of the side which is twisted upwards, and this has to be planed parallel with the top edge of the other side. These

corrections will make the drawer run freely, but they will not necessarily bring the front flush with its opening. To do this it may be necessary to plane or scrape off the projecting portion and this often involves removing the handles. If there is a key escutcheon in the area to be planed, the lock can be removed and the escutcheon tapped out. To avoid the risk of splintering the drawer front, a small block of wood, with the shape of the escutcheon cut out of it, is pressed against the wood surrounding the escutcheon while it is being tapped out. If there is not much wood to be removed it is better to leave the escutcheon in position and cut the wood and the brass with abrasive paper.

Damaged surfaces

If a hard surface, like matt polyurethane, is lightly scratched it can be sanded down, re-lacquered and lightly rubbed with wire wool. But if the surface of the wood is damaged, the film of lacquer has to be removed with a scraper and the wood smoothed with fine abrasive paper before being re-lacquered. It is difficult to merge a re-lacquered patch into the surrounding area and if there are many marks and scratches on a table top it is better to scrape the whole surface down to the wood and make a fresh start.

Waxed surfaces are often damaged by hot cups or spilled liquids. If the wax has been applied over a hard lacquered surface it can be cleaned off with turpentine and replaced. But if the wax has been applied directly to the furniture, the wood itself is liable to be stained and to need re-surfacing with fine abrasive paper before the wax is replaced.

List of Addresses

UK

Hand tools are available from DIY and hardware shops, and large department stores. In case of difficulty in obtaining any tool, the following Association will provide information on availability:

The Federation of British Hand Tools Association
Light Trades House
Melbourne Avenue
Sheffield S10 2QJ

All types of wood and veneers are available from reputable timber merchants, and their addresses may be found in local telephone directories. In case of difficulty in obtaining a particular type of wood, the Branch Secretaries of the Timber Trades Federation will provide information on availability:

London Area Timber Association
Clareville House
Whitcomb Street
London WC2H 7DL

North East Coast Timber Trade Association
Pearl Assurance House
7 New Bridge Street
Newcastle-upon-Tyne NE1 8BQ

Bristol Channel Timber Trades Association
27 Heol Hir
Llanishen
Cardiff CF4 5AA

Scottish Timber Trade Association
402 Sauchiehall Street
Glasgow G2 3JH

Northern Ireland Timber Importers Association
2 Greenwood Avenue
Belfast 4

Irish Timber Importers Association
Crescent Trust Co
Gardner House
Ballsbridge
Dublin 4

Information on the properties and behaviour of particular types of wood can be obtained from the Timber Research and Development Association:

TRADA
Hughenden Valley
High Wycombe
Buckinghamshire HP14 4ND

USA

Advice on buying timber may be obtained from:

The Federal Timber Purchasers Association
3900 South Wadsworth Blvd
201 Denver
Colorado 80235

Bibliography

Books
Desch, H E, *Timber – Its Structure and Properties,* Macmillan & Co Ltd (revised edition 1968)
Hayward, Charles H, *The Complete Book of Woodwork,* Evans Brothers, 1955 (revised edition 1974)
Hayward, Charles H, *Woodwork Joints,* Evans Brothers, 1950 (revised edition 1975)
Joyce, Ernest, *The Technique of Furniture Making,* B T Batsford Ltd, 1970 (revised edition 1974)

Magazines and journals
UK
Timber and Plywood Telephone Address Book, Middlesex Publishing Co Ltd, 21 New Street, London EC2
Woodworker and *Woodworker Annual,* Model and Allied Publications Ltd, 13–35 Bridge Street, Hemel Hempstead, Herts
Practical Woodworking, IPC Magazines Ltd, Fleetway House, Farringdon Street, London EC4
Do It Yourself, Link House Publications Ltd, Link House, Dingwall Avenue, Croydon

USA
Woodworking and Furniture Digest, Hitchcock Publishing Co, Wheaton, Illinois 60187

Index